ENDORSEMENTS

Carolyn Kerr's book, *Lift Up Your Head: Joy in the Face of Shame* is outstanding! It deals with an important and difficult topic which is too often neglected both in the church and in the secular world. Kerr points out how debilitating yet how common shame is. This is an essential work for pastors, therapists, counselors and anyone who has ever been made to feel ashamed.

Rev. Dr. Paul Leggett, Pastor
Grace Presbyterian Church, Montrose, N.J.

Lift Up Your Head: Joy in the Face of Shame gives the reader unique insights into the often neglected consideration of the presence of shame. Carolyn Kerr ventures into the murky waters of the painful reality which exists for many of us. In so doing, she establishes an invaluable foundation as to the nature of shame, the differences between shame and guilt, plus ways to overcome this highly restrictive hazard. Dr. Kerr is particularly qualified to deal with this sticky subject—a solid psychological education and a biblical orientation; vast cross-cultural experience; and years in counseling ministry. This book helps fill a void in psychology and Christian literature. It is essential reading for Christians, clergy, counselors and professors in the field.

Clayton L. ("Mike") Berg, Jr., LHD
Retired president of the Latin America Mission

This is a good and helpful book . . . . I am really pleased with it.

Dr. Charles H. Kraft, Senior Professor
School of Intercultural Studies, Fuller Theological Seminary

Carolyn Kerr has produced a valuable work on a topic which does not get as much attention as it should. Since the primary cause of missionary attrition is interpersonal difficulties, materials of this kind are extremely valuable to mission societies doing member care work.

Her use of Jesus' incarnation is especially helpful. She states, "Jesus did not depend upon public opinion to know who he was." She talks about the shock he must have felt when he left heaven and came to earth, the terrible treatment he received in general, the support he had from John the Baptist, and the complete dependence on the truth and on God the Father that enabled him to carry out his mission. He modeled for us life and ministry free of shame.

I recommend this book to anyone struggling with this phenomenon whether on a personal level or as one tasked with the care of others.

Rex Lee Carlaw
USA Director and International Council Chairman
Action International Ministries

LIFT UP YOUR HEAD

*Joy
in the
Face of
Shame*

Carolyn E. Kerr

WestBow
PRESS
A DIVISION OF THOMAS NELSON

Scripture taken from THE HOLY BIBLE, NEW INTERNATIONAL VERSION, Copyright 1973, 1978, 1984 by International Bible Society. Used by permission of Zondervan. All rights reserved.

WestBow Press books may be ordered through booksellers or by contacting:

WestBow Press
A Division of Thomas Nelson
1663 Liberty Drive
Bloomington, IN 47403
www.westbowpress.com
1-(866) 928-1240

Because of the dynamic nature of the Internet, any web addresses or links contained in this book may have changed since publication and may no longer be valid. The views expressed in this work are solely those of the author and do not necessarily reflect the views of the publisher, and the publisher hereby disclaims any responsibility for them.

Any people depicted in stock imagery provided by Thinkstock are models, and such images are being used for illustrative purposes only.

Certain stock imagery © Thinkstock.

ISBN: 978-1-4497-5167-8 (sc)
ISBN: 978-1-4497-5168-5 (hc)
ISBN: 978-1-4497-5166-1 (e)

Library of Congress Control Number: 2012908332

Printed in the United States of America

WestBow Press rev. date: 05/07/2012

For Carlos,
who wondered if it wasn't really pride after all.
I'm sorry the answer was so long in coming.

For Cassy – that you can forgive
yourself
and
for Cami, that you can forgive.
others because you are forgiven
Carolyn Kerr

If I am guilty—woe to me! Even if I am innocent, I cannot lift my head,
for I am full of shame and drowned in my affliction.
Job 10:15

But you are a shield around me, O Lord;
you bestow glory on me and lift up my head.
Psalm 3:3

Jesus, . . . for the joy set before him endured the cross, scorning the shame . . .
Hebrews 12:2

Contents

Acknowledgments

If I tried to make an exhaustive list of all those who have encouraged me, given me ideas, challenged my concepts, and corrected my style and grammar, it would occupy pages and pages and even so I would be sure to leave out someone important.

The seemingly interminable evolution of this book into its present form has taken more than twelve years. During that time I have "tried it out" on a large number of people, whose comments and suggestions have helped mold the result. Those who come after them will surely benefit from their experience.

Four people do need to be acknowledged by name. I am grateful to Jane Campbell of Chosen Books who gave me very helpful editorial advice. My sister-in-law, Martha St. John Kerr, did a marvelous job of proofreading. I guarantee that if you find any errors in spelling or grammar they were introduced by changes made after she operated on the manuscript. Thanks also to my son, Andy Kerr, who advised me on artistic matters.

Especially I wish to thank my husband, Edwin Lewis Kerr, for his continual encouragement, availability to talk over ideas, and technical help. Without him, I surely would have stashed the book in a file somewhere in the sub-basement of my computer and given up on it long ago.

Introduction

Have you ever had the sensation that you were all wrong? Not that you had made an error or done something wrong, necessarily, but that you were precisely what you didn't want to be? Have you ever felt like you desperately wanted to disappear into a hole, somewhere where nobody could find you? Do you hesitate to let other people know what you are really like inside because you are afraid if you do they might not like you?

Everybody has these feelings once in a while, because we all have a certain amount of shame in our lives. But some people live with that kind of pain on a daily basis. And when the pain of shame is chronic, it is often undeserved, the result of being shamed by other people.

Shame hurts. When I was a kid I never did figure out what was wrong with me, why I was always the last person chosen for anything, why the others formed their exclusive clubs and left me out, why they snickered at me. Then I found that I could do well in school, and that made the teachers like me, at least. That was exactly the wrong strategy to get friends among my classmates, of course. I became a loner, not because I wanted to be, but to protect myself from more pain. Shame can lead to depression, and all through my time in high school I was struggling with suicidal thoughts.

Obviously I didn't kill myself. I stumbled on a way out of my shame through a personal relationship with the living Jesus Christ. I didn't really understand much of what was going on in my own life at that time. Years later after having helped others to find faith and freedom, and after getting my doctorate in clinical psychology, I began to connect the dots. My motive in writing this book is to reach out to others who may be stumbling around like I was, and point them to a path to freedom from shame.

Or maybe you don't feel much shame yourself, but you have to live with or work with people who do. That can also be pretty uncomfortable, especially if you don't see that they are suffering, because it sure looks to you like they are proud and controlling. This book may also help you to discern better what is going on with some of your "high maintenance relationships".

It is my prayer that this book may be a means for healing and refreshment to those who read it.

C.E.K.

CHAPTER 1 | The Great Cover-up

When I was ten years old, I asked my parents for some ice skates for Christmas. I had seen other kids happily skating on the frozen pond that was just a few blocks from our house, and it looked like fun.

The skates appeared under the tree, but then I had a problem. I didn't know how to skate. I don't know if my parents could skate or not, but they didn't offer to teach me, or even give me any pointers. I went out into the back yard where there were some puddles frozen over and put the skates on, but there didn't seem to be any point to that. Finally I just went over to the pond.

I had never gotten very close to the pond before, so this was a new experience. The closer I got, the slower I walked. What would be the attitude of the other kids when they found out I didn't know how to skate? How could I stand their laughter when I fell down (because I knew for sure I would fall)? When I was within view of the skating pond I stopped behind a tree where nobody could see me and watched the other kids. They could all skate well. Some were playing hockey. I stood behind the tree for a quarter of an hour or so trying to work up the nerve to come out, but there was no way I could make myself get any closer. I went home and put the skates away. I would skate for the first time some fifteen years later, after going through a long struggle with myself and the shame that bound me.

Shame doesn't always look like that, though. A bully, a sweet lady who is always helping others, a show-off in a red convertible who doesn't believe the traffic laws apply to him, a guy who always has to win every argument, a perfect housekeeper, and a wit with a nasty insulting comeback may all be suffering from shame.

Shame is a painful emotion that comes from believing that you are deficient, or not what you should be. Something is lacking— perhaps something that really can't be expressed in words. If you feel shame you "know" that you are inadequate, that you can't do it (whatever "it" is), that you are no good. Something inside you tells you that you are not acceptable. When you think about yourself, you can't be happy with what you see. You are ashamed of yourself.

This feeling often has nothing to do with the reality that other people see. People who are capable, beautiful, intelligent and popular can believe themselves to be clumsy, ugly, stupid and rejected. Women especially are vulnerable to feeling shame. We'll deal with some of the reasons for this shortly.

Even if you feel a lot of shame, things may not be too bad while other people are affirming you and expressing their approval, though you may have a hard time believing these affirmations. Even so, the fact that you get along with everyone won't even touch your interior feeling of insecurity. If anyone criticizes you (particularly in public) or if someone makes you look ridiculous, the pain is almost beyond bearing. The problem is not just that you have difficulty in relating to the people who criticize you. The problem comes from your relationship with yourself. If you were sure of yourself the opinion of others wouldn't matter so much. But if you suffer from shame the question, "What will people think?" can have immense importance, to the point that this worry can become your jailer.

Some call this lack of confidence in oneself *low self-esteem*. But that term doesn't really explain where the low opinion comes from. Generally it comes from a tendency to feel shame in many situations.

One would think that shame was so common that everyone would know what it is. Even so there is a lot of confusion about it. For instance we confuse it with the uncomfortable feeling we have when we get into an embarrassing situation. Shame and embarrassment are different in two ways. First, embarrassment usually occurs only when other people are aware of what is going on, but shame can hit at any time, even in private. Second, shame is more intense than mere embarrassment. I might get red in the face if I drip some soup on the front of my blouse during a dinner with important people. I might be uncomfortable if I can't remember the words I need in a conversation. Once when I went to introduce my brother to someone I forgot his name!

But these embarrassing moments do not usually cause the strong, almost unbearable pain that shame does. In the case of embarrassment I become uncomfortable because other people can see me and might think badly of me. Embarrassment is both social and public. Shame, however, is an interior matter that is felt even in private—even if other people aren't looking.

The psychologist Michael Lewis has done some research on the difference between shame and embarrassment. He has shown that embarrassment is relatively superficial, but shame is deep pain. Sometimes you can see the difference in people's actions. People who are ashamed sometimes look like they wish to hide, disappear, or die. Embarrassed people, however, will often look in multiple directions and then look away with a small smile. Hardly ever will a person who feels shame look away and smile.

Let's return to my experience with those ice skates. Supposing that I had managed to get to the skating pond, put on my skates, and stagger out onto the ice—only to fall down almost immediately. Without a load of shame in my life, I would probably have bruised my pride as well as my elbows, but I would have been able to laugh a little, get back up and try again. With shame, though, even if the other kids were pleasant and helpful, a little voice inside my head would tell me I was making a complete fool of myself and make me want to just sink into the ice and disappear.

The shame we are talking about is not natural timidity, something that some people seem to have right from infancy. A timid temperament may be a physiological matter, hard-wired by genetics, and not the result of things that happen in life.

People also confuse shame and guilt, using the words as though they were synonyms. In order to describe either shame or guilt, people say they feel "bad", because both are painful. Shame and guilt are sometimes called "moral emotions" because of their relationship with cultural values and morality.

But they aren't the same thing. Guilt is a reaction we have after having done something we know we shouldn't have done (or after having left undone something we know we ought to have done). Guilt is directly related to our actions. We recognize that we have behaved badly and we are motivated to repair the damage, pay our debt to the victim if any, and make sure it doesn't happen again.

Shame can also be a reaction to something which we have done, or even to some negative situation. But with shame, the focus is not on what we have done, but rather on ourselves. "Because of what I have done I am a bad person". Or the reverse, "I did something bad because I am a bad person. Everyone will know that I am bad. I want to have the earth swallow me up so I can disappear. I feel small. I want to escape, flee from the other person or the situation. Instead of wanting to fix the damage, I want to cover it up, to hide my part in what happened". The pain of shame is intense.

Or it might be that you haven't done anything wrong at all, but rather you are suffering from undeserved shame—shame you have acquired from others. We can't be sure to what point the shame we feel is deserved. Some people constantly accuse themselves of everything and others don't recognize that all of us have dark and hidden parts where unsuspected things lurk.

You might feel guilt or shame as a reaction to any negative situation. Often whether you feel guilt or shame depends more on the habit you have formed of experiencing one or the other than it does on the situation itself. It doesn't depend on whether someone is watching you or not.

For example, suppose I have used the self-checkout lane at the supermarket, then discover when I get to my car that there were some items left in my cart that I didn't pass through the scanner and didn't pay for. I recognize my error. If I am motivated by guilt I will be sure to go to the customer service desk, explain what happened, and pay what I owe.. Guilt serves to keep me honest.

But perhaps besides feeling guilt, I also tell myself that I am a thief, that I am stupid for not being able to use the system right, or something like that. I desperately hope that nobody saw me walk out without paying, but even if they didn't see me I have my own private shame. If I have someone with me, the possibility of feeling shame grows because of the spectators. But it is guilt that makes me pay up.

Suppose Nancy is telling jokes with some friends while having coffee in a busy cafe. The name of another friend, Rosa, comes up, and Nancy's friends start talking badly about Rosa. Nancy wants to get on well with her friends, so she tells a true story about Rosa that shows up many of her faults. Everyone laughs. If Nancy realizes that she has betrayed her friend she may feel either guilt or shame. If she feels *guilt*, she recognizes that she has acted badly. She will think of Rosa and the damage she has done to her name, and will want to correct the situation. She will tell her friends to forget what she said, because Rosa is her friend and she shouldn't have spoken badly of her. But if Nancy feels *shame*, she will feel very small. She will be thinking of herself—not of Rosa—and will consider that she is a failure as a friend. If she says anything to her current companions, it may be to change the subject, and they will never know what she is thinking. It is not the presence of her companions that inspires the shame, but rather her own thoughts.

Now think about what happens if when they get up they find that Rosa is sitting at the next table and could have overheard their conversation. Nancy will feel "bad", of course. If what she feels is *guilt*, she will think about Rosa and the pain that she must be feeling. She might sit down immediately with Rosa and ask for forgiveness, or even call the other friends, confess her fault, and invite them to be reconciled to Rosa also—if Rosa will allow it. It is even possible that the relationship between Nancy and Rosa might be saved. But if what Nancy feels is *shame* she will get out of there as fast as possible, hiding her face and pretending she hasn't seen Rosa. Her friendship with Rosa is probably over.

As another example, suppose that while I am in a friend's house I accidently knock a vase off of a table and the fall chips the edge a bit. I feel "bad" of course, but if the bad feeling is *guilt* I will go to my friend, confess what happened and offer to fix or replace the vase. Guilt will motivate me to think of my friend. Shame, on the contrary, makes me think of myself. If I am motivated by *shame*, I may try to stick the piece back on a bit, turn the vase so it doesn't show, and pretend nothing happened. Eventually the friend will discover the broken vase, of course, but by then it may not be evident that I did it. Meanwhile I suffer within, not only because of the vase but because of the deception, and I start avoiding my friend. Besides breaking the vase, I may have broken the relationship, which is part of what I feared when I tried to cover up my mistake.

Ruth was dismayed at how much a seemingly insignificant memory was troubling her. More than fifty years before, she had borrowed a book from a friend and taken it with her on a trip. Apparently when she went to get off of an airplane she didn't check the seat pocket in front of her and left the book. Later the airline didn't know anything about it. Ruth was not poor and could have replaced the book with no trouble, but instead she yielded to her shame. She let some time lapse, and when her friend asked about the book Ruth said she had returned it already, didn't the friend remember? The friend didn't remember, but Ruth did. Fifty years later her face got red as she spoke of it. In her shame she wanted to cover up what had happened, but her guilt continued to bother her. It was now too late to make amends to the friend, who had died. And in addition to her original shame, now she had the additional shame of knowing that she was indeed the kind of person who would lie to cover up an accidental fault with a lie and defraud her friend.

But it is not necessary for us to have done something wrong in order to feel guilt or shame. These feelings can be the result of the way people have treated us, or from rules that we have been taught, for example that we have to be perfect or nobody will love us.

We can even feel guilt or shame for what others have done, although this normally is limited to people with whom we identify deeply. Parents of a child arrested for shoplifting may feel guilt (for not have watched or disciplined better their child) or shame (for being bad parents).

Guilt is concerned with something you did, and motivates you to do what you have to do in order to make the situation right. *Shame* makes you think that you yourself are a bad person and motivates you to cover up the situation. *Guilt* is specific, related with a specific thing. *Shame* is global, making you think you are all bad instead of just focusing on a specific area of your life.

Guilt may not last very long, since it disappears if you confess what you did and make restitution and are forgiven. The pain of *shame* may last indefinitely, returning years later whenever you recall the incident.

For many years psychologists and psychiatrists have insisted that guilt is bad. Many books and articles have been written about the damage that guilt does to people. I have read numerous times that being a Christian is bad for you since Christianity teaches people to feel guilt. But according to research in the past 20 years or so, it turns out that guilt isn't so bad. The research of June Price Tangney, source of some of the examples of shame in this book, has demonstrated that in reality feeling guilt is good for the individual and for society.

Now why is that? Since guilt just tells you that you have done something wrong, but doesn't attack who you are at heart, it does not make you think you are a bad person. It doesn't become globalized to all parts of your life. And it motivates you to repent, make it right and try to do better in the future. The tendency to feel guilt instead of shame as a reaction to a negative incident produces better mental health and better interpersonal relationships. It is also good for society in general that people react with guilt when they have done wrong, not only because there will be more emotionally healthy people but so the crime rate will be lower.

On the other hand, shame has long been considered to be good, an instrument to get us to change our behavior. Someone who takes advantage of others is said to be "shameless", and that marks the person as bad. But the research of Tangney and others has shown that shame does not help us refrain from doing bad things, does not move us to repentance or restitution. Instead, habitually feeling shame is related to poor mental health, low self-esteem, depression, and poorer quality in our relationships with others.

Everyone feels guilt and shame from time to time, but the research of Tangney has shown that each person has a "preferred" style. It seems that people have their own personal habits of thinking and feeling, and tend to react in the same manner in many situations. Those who habitually feel shame she has termed "shame prone", which is what they will be called in this book.

Lewis Smedes, whom I had the privilege of knowing and with whom I studied in seminary, wrote in his book, *Shame and Grace: Healing the Shame We Don't Deserve,* that some people are more likely candidates for feeling shame than others, specifically:

Guilt Spreaders who allow the guilt from one thing to contaminate their whole being. If they make a mess of something, they automatically conclude that everything about them is bad. Their motto might be, "I did, therefore I am."

The Overly Responsible. They, not God, have the whole world in their hands, and they are responsible to fix it. At least they think so, whether other people see it that way or not.

Obsessive Moralizers. Everything we do has to be right or wrong. Nothing is slightly bad or slightly good. Nothing is just for fun. Violating a custom is the same as breaking the law.

Compulsive Comparers. They compare themselves with successful people and consider themselves failures when a friend has a triumph. They feel like they have to be better than everyone else at everything they do.

Approval Addicts. They never get enough approval to fill their need. They especially long for the approval of their parents.

The Never Deserving. They don't deserve anything and they can't enjoy it when they get it. They may feel "guilty" when something good happens to them.

People Condemned by Bad Memories. Everyone has hurt others at some time or another, but these people remember all of those times and think about them regularly.

Those Who Dwell in the Shadows of Their Parents. Whether they were good or bad, the children always feel their influence.

People Who Feel Condemned by Their Dreams. Not everything we dream about is true!

Shame-prone people have some counterproductive ways of thinking about themselves. If you are shame-prone, in your own thoughts, you tend to discount anything positive about yourself. When you hear someone else say something in your favor, you discount it quickly before it can influence your way of thinking about yourself. If you do this, receiving compliments can't change the way you think or feel. Having many successes doesn't help because you will always find some way of showing yourself that the successes mean nothing. You want success, not to help the world, but just to feel good. But it doesn't help in the long run. If you have not had an overwhelming success, it feels like a failure. Any imperfection is enough to make you feel totally bad. If you do one thing wrong, it seems like proof that you are worthless.

Mike wanted some help with his depression. He certainly looked sad and tired, and he told about just wanting to stay in bed all day, and crying at the least provocation. When I asked how long this had been going on, he said that he had always been a little bit that way. I wondered then why he had waited until then to get help. The symptoms had gotten worse in the last couple of weeks, he said, ever since he failed the qualifying exams for the profession he had trained for. He considered himself a complete failure. Explaining to him that a lot of people fail those exams the first time, and that he could take them again did not fix the situation. Mentioning to him the various accomplishments and good qualities he had made no difference in his assessment that he was totally bad. He was completely ashamed of himself. He had always had a tendency to discount anything others said was good about him, and had a habit of running himself down, but this latest blow clinched the deal. He was no good at all, not just the part of him that failed the exams. Shame is global.

If shame-prone people are criticized, they take it as a judgment on their whole being, a total condemnation. This could produce a profound sadness in some, causing them to retreat into a shell. In others, it could produce a furious explosion, damaging everyone available, friend and foe. It is possible that shame-prone people could explode emotionally even if nobody has specifically criticized them, because they tend to believe that other people share their own low opinion of them. It is possible that they might recognize that their way of thinking doesn't connect well with reality, but it is very difficult for them to change. Indeed, without help they can't change.

To make thinking badly of themselves even worse, shame-prone people also tend to think constantly about themselves and their own welfare. They give themselves a constant dose of negativity about themselves. The condemnation just doesn't let up.

When we feel shame, we would do almost anything to get rid of the pain inside. We try to protect ourselves so that we don't feel the pain so much. We also want to keep others from discovering what we feel, and especially keep them from shaming us even more. The result of this protectionism is that we think about ourselves most of the time. If we are self-centered like that we will have a hard time relating to other people, since they will expect us to think about them, too.

The ability to appreciate what other people are feeling is called empathy. It helps you act selflessly, have warm relationships with others, and avoid aggression. It also helps you understand others' situations and think about helping those who are suffering some pain or injustice. Empathy is necessary for a happy family. It turns out that shame inhibits empathy, according to Tangney's research. It causes you to concentrate on your own experiences and needs instead of on those of others. Instead of responding to others with empathy you focus on yourself. That means that shame gets in the way of relating well to other people. It messes up our families; it keeps us from being helpful, useful members of a community.

In order to really unite our lives with others, we have to share our world with them. We have to tear down the wall that separates us and be willing for others to know us. But if we feel a lot of shame, that thought makes us afraid. Who knows if other people will understand and accept us?

John Powell treats this problem in a masterful little book called, *"Why Am I Afraid to Tell You Who I Am?"* His answer is, "I am afraid to tell you who I am, because if I do you may not like who I am, and it is all I have." But if we don't share who we are, we remain isolated and not understood. The person who is understood and loved will grow as a person. The isolated person will wither away.

So how do you go about this business of protecting yourself from the pain of shame? There are three basic strategies which you could use. One is to get rid of the norms, the rules that say what we must be and do in order to be acceptable, so that there won't be any contradiction between them and our self-concept. If there is no difference between what we think we should be and what we think we are, we will not feel the hurt and will have no shame. Another solution is to know and confess the reality of what we are or what we have done and receive forgiveness and acceptance from the Lord and from other people. The third way is to cover up the feeling of shame along with its cause.

Some psychologists have recommended the first way, getting rid of the norms. If there are no rules, there won't be any shame or guilt because there can't be any contrast between what we are and what we should be. There are many difficulties with this strategy. One is that we all have an inner sense of what is right, and it is difficult to convince ourselves (and, perhaps, a judge and jury) that it is all right to do whatever we might like. Another problem is that if everyone adopted this way of treating shame, society would rapidly be converted into a jungle of lies, deceptions, robberies, broken relationships, injustices and violence. Some people think we have already arrived at this point.

In the case of undeserved shame, when others have made rules according to their fancy and have judged us unjustly, we could try to get out of our heads the false laws such as "you have to be perfect so they will accept you" or "you aren't allowed to have your own opinions." We could then act with more freedom. But it is very difficult for anyone to recognize which of the rules they believe in are unhealthy in order to get rid of them, especially since the rules have become habits of thinking, a part of who they are. We need help and support from a community where we feel accepted to get this freedom.

The second strategy, open confession of the truth, is a road which can take us to freedom from the consequences of guilt and shame, but it is a difficult road for someone who feels shame. A shamed person wants to cover up, not confess. In the case of merited shame, in which we also have guilt, confession and repentance are the conditions to receiving God's forgiveness and starting over. When we suffer from undeserved shame, confession is a process of telling the truth about ourselves and the situation. It doesn't necessarily reveal anything bad that we have done.

It is very freeing to be able to admit to ourselves and another person who will hear us with love and acceptance whatever it is that we are feeling and why. But freeing as this is, truly shamed people will not be able to bring themselves to take these steps, at least by themselves. We will get back to this in later chapters of the book.

Given the difficulties of eliminating the rules and opening their inner thoughts to others' inspection, people generally tend to choose the third strategy for protecting themselves, which is covering up. We deny the feelings of shame and fear, so that nobody will see the weakness and either bring it out in the open or take advantage of us. Sometimes we use silence as a defense, ensuring that nobody knows what is inside. Sometimes we use intellectual arguments to distance other people, so that they won't get too close and guess what is there.

Shame is an interior phenomenon; invisible from outside and sometimes denied from inside, even when it is there. The more that we deny it and cover it up, the more it can affect us without being detected. The face we put to the public can sometimes become real to us, too, and help us to ignore what is under the surface. In protecting ourselves by covering our shame from other people, we may keep ourselves from seeing it also.

There are basically two ways to cover up shame. The Swiss physician Paul Tournier describes them very well in his book, *The Strong and the Weak*, although he is not there specifically talking about shame. One cover-up is the "strong" or "hard" method, most often practiced by men (though women do it, too). The other is the "soft" or "weak" method which women prefer. Neither is exclusive to men or to women, but there are preferences. The two ways of covering our shame differ from each other, but they have in common the purpose of protecting us from the pain of shame and from possible attacks from people who would shame us even more. The following descriptions present the two attitudes in an exaggerated way in order to make the difference obvious. In reality few people are such extremists.

The strong or hard cover-up

The strong cover-up involves trying to control circumstances and other people so as to be sure that we won't be shamed again. People who use this strategy act as though they felt strong (giving orders to others, for example), innocent (condemning the conduct of others and criticizing them), invincible (imposing their will on others), confident (putting other people down and shaming them), and perfect in every sense.

Supposedly this proclaims to everyone that they are master not only of themselves but also of anyone who comes close. It is a false image because what they really feel is the reverse.

They feel weak, without power, ignorant, and clumsy. They hope to fool everyone else and hopefully themselves also. They are afraid that someone might discover what they really are, or that they might look weak or ridiculous or dependent. They may react strongly to criticism and even to an indirect suggestion that they might not be perfect, since these show that there is a hole in their armor.

This way of dealing with shame is perceived from outside as pride. If you have to interact with someone like this you might think that they have an excess of self-esteem, but the truth is the opposite. The supposed strong man who struts about imposing his will on others doesn't feel high self-esteem. He feels threatened. He is afraid of being ridiculed.

Those who use the strong cover-up can never admit to any weakness, not to themselves, nor to others. They cannot stand it when someone takes advantage of them, not only for the obvious loss, but also because this shows that they didn't know how to defend themselves. Inside, they want to avoid weakness at all cost, because weakness leads to being shamed more.

They have to be the best at everything: the most brilliant student, the most successful salesman, the most celebrated musician, the athlete with the most new records, the politician with the most votes, the most beautiful model. They are not the backup act, but always the main attraction. It is not sufficient to be like everybody else. They have to be outstanding.

They never admit to being wrong or having made a mistake. They are always right, even though the evidence shows that they aren't. They may have to think for a bit to come up with some twisted reasoning to justify themselves, but they can do it.

They tend to blame others for everything that goes wrong in their own life and around them. Bob said he wanted some help, not for himself, but for his family. He said his wife, Terri, was bad-tempered, disorganized, lazy, a spendthrift, and kept a dirty house. She didn't discipline the children, who were disrespectful and doing poorly in school because they wasted all their time with their friends and didn't study. Terri and their teenage children agreed to talk about this. They pointed out that Bob himself came home late each evening in a bad mood and started yelling at everyone, without making any attempt to help anyone. Bob explained his behavior by saying that his boss made his life unbearable with his unreasonable demands, and that he needed to go out for a drink with his buddies after work to unwind. The youngest son pointed out that his dad was doing the same thing to them that his boss did to him, but Bob couldn't see it that way. When his son dared to make this suggestion it produced an explosion of anger from Bob. What he was doing was justified, but what they and his boss were doing was not.

If at any time the person does appear to be guilty of something, he may react strongly to anyone who accuses him. He will reverse the accusation, furiously, with a level of emotion which is much greater than that which the situation would seem to call for. He will become even more furious if he himself has to acknowledge that his accusations against the other person are not justified. He wants to make sure that the guilt doesn't stick on him, but rather on the other person. He could become aggressive, either directly or indirectly.

If he manages to get the guilt transferred to the other person, a kind of justified anger will enable him to recover the sensation of controlling the situation. Anger is an emotion that brings with it a sensation of force and authority. In contrast, shame is an emotion considered to belong to weak and cowardly people.

If the person feels shamed, lessened in front of others, he looks for a way to blame someone else for his experience of the pain of shame.

They are guilty because they have shamed him. The accused other people may not even have been evaluating him badly in their own minds or intentions, but that is unimportant. What is important is what he thinks the others are thinking.

For the other people around him, this anger appears as something inexplicable that has fallen on them. It is not rational. If they respond to the anger by protecting themselves with their own anger, resentment, or denial of the charges against them, the anger of the accuser will likely increase to the point of fury.

If the others don't respond at all, even this lack of response may generate fury. If he realizes that he has responded more strongly than the situation demands, this interior recognition makes him feel even more shamed. The increasing shame motivates him to feel more anger to cover it up, and there is no way to stop the spiral toward fury.

Fury is more serious than simple anger. Fury is a state in which the person feels powerless (in itself an unbearable situation) and out of control. The original object of the anger sometimes is lost and the fury is directed at everything and everyone in general.

For several years I taught counseling in a school for preparing Christian workers. The director of the school was a man with some administrative ability, but no academic preparation and no talent for teaching. Among the teachers under his supervision were several people with stellar qualifications. As time went on it became evident that the director was afraid that the better prepared teachers would at some point revolt against his management, so the rules about what could and could not be done became ever more strict and numerous.

There came an evening when I was teaching on shame and its effects. To illustrate the fury of a thwarted shamed person using the hard style of defense, I gave a reasonable imitation of a rant, "I'm in charge here! What I say is the way things will be! I don't care what anyone else wants done or says. I'm the boss!" I was surprised at the incredibly shocked expression on the faces of all of the students, especially when I had taken the precaution of explaining that it was an illustration, and I had not raised my voice. I didn't find out until after class what was going on.

It turned out that the night before one of the other teachers had changed his class program around a bit. The director had heard about it and didn't like it, and so had come into the class and denounced the other teacher in front of the class in a voice that could be heard outside the building, saying almost word for word what I had just said. My students suddenly realized what they had experienced the night before. I am sorry to say that their admiration for the director was somewhat less after that.

Albert Camus' novel, *The Fall*, is an extended monologue by a character who exhibits many of the symptoms of shame. He describes the need to be right in these terms:

"But, after all, I was on the right side; that was enough to satisfy my conscience. The feeling of the law, the satisfaction of being right, the joy of self-esteem, *cher monsieur*, are powerful incentives for keeping us upright or keeping us moving forward. On the other hand, if you deprive men of them, you transform them into dogs frothing with rage. How many crimes committed merely because their authors could not endure being wrong! I once knew a manufacturer who had a perfect wife, admired by all, and yet he deceived her. That man was literally furious to be in the wrong, to be blocked from receiving, or granting himself, a certificate of virtue. The more virtues his wife manifested, the more vexed he became. Eventually, living in the wrong became unbearable to him. What do you think he did then? He gave up deceiving her? Not at all. He killed her."

Anger itself is not bad. Even Jesus was angered by the money changers in the temple. God gets angry about sin. Nevertheless there are good and bad ways to manage our anger. Anger, well directed and focused on a problem to solve it, can have very positive results in the end. Badly used, and when it degenerates to fury, it can make someone hostile and aggressive, possibly messing up permanently what could have been long-term relationships.

The weak or soft cover-up

The soft or weak cover-up used to protect oneself from the pain of shame looks very different. It is not so much characterized by swagger and aggression as by the tendency to exaggerate your own faults, serve others, and be what others want you to be. It is more likely to make you sad than to make you angry. Most people who use the weak cover-up don't try to dominate others directly, but they can be very manipulative.

Weak defenders tend to adjust their lives so that they are what other people want them to be. They adopt the opinions, the preferences, and the habits of others.

Shirley and her husband had recently moved into a new apartment, and the budget would allow them to have new furniture for the living room. Shirley really liked Danish Modern style, and her husband said he didn't care, whatever she wanted was all right with him. She had found a set she wanted to buy at a local furniture store. One morning when she and a friend went out for coffee, she asked the friend to come to the store with her to see what she had picked out. As they walked into the store, the friend exclaimed enthusiastically about a French Provincial set that was near the door. Shirley let her talk on without making any comment herself. Later as they were coming to Shirley's favorite, the friend pointed to it and laughed at how ugly it was. She said not only were the colors atrocious, but it looked so incredibly uncomfortable. Shirley ended up buying the French Provincial set that her friend liked, though in the years to come she never felt like the living room was really hers. Having to please everyone is a terrifically heavy burden.

There are techniques for winning friends and influencing people by saying and doing things that make others feel appreciated. They work. The reason they work is that everyone wants to be accepted. But applying the technique and getting other people to say they like you doesn't take away the fear inside. Besides, manipulating people like that produces neither love nor long-lasting relationships. The Bible says that perfect love casts out fear (I John 4:18). The reverse is also true. Fear makes it very difficult to love someone, that is, to act in the real best interests of the other person instead of just using them to make ourselves feel better. Sooner or later our self-centeredness will come out, and the person who has been manipulated or deceived will not be happy about it. Using the techniques is usually just a short-term patch on the problem of trying to be accepted, since it is difficult to behave for a long time as though we were better than we really are.

Those who choose the weak strategy, especially if they are women, tend to advertise their faults instead of hiding them. In most parts of the world it is part of "feminine culture" to avoid praising oneself, since that would be a sign of pride. This is also true in some church groups. It is fairly common to hear a woman say that she is clumsy, that she doesn't understand complicated things, that she isn't much good at this or that.

For a couple of years I took a course in lagartera embroidery in a little town in Spain near where we lived. This type of embroidery is rather difficult, and the beginner sometimes gets the feeling that she rips out more stitches than she puts in. There was a woman in the class who always decried her clumsiness and complained loudly each time she made a mistake. The other women felt the obligation to contradict her and appreciate what she was doing right, even more so because she really was a bit clumsy. Besides just contradicting the claims of the woman, each one would show her own errors and say that in reality she herself was the most worthless. It was sort of a contest to see who could be the clumsiest.

Although declaring one's own faults seems a bit counterproductive as a method of getting rid of shame, it works in the short run because it is only done in the presence of people who know that they should contradict the negative confession. This can produce some very positive results if it is done right and others are disposed to cooperate. The person criticizes herself, not out of true humility and being content with who she is, but as a way to receive praise from others. She exaggerates her faults, probably without realizing what she is doing, so that people will tell her that she is all right, that they accept her. This is not the same as confessing a real fault and being forgiven. A woman operating in this exaggerated fault mode would be extremely hurt if anyone took her confessions at face value.

A woman who spends five hours a day cleaning her house but asks guests to please excuse the mess knows that her house is all right. The protests of her guests serve to make her feel better about herself. Also if there is anything that has escaped her diligence, it is covered under her confession, because she is making it known that she has very high norms for herself even if she doesn't always reach them. Even if the house isn't perfect, she is. If she is to be judged she will be found faultless.

The narrator in *The Fall* by Albert Camus is deeply controlled by shame. At one point after he has been confessing some of the things he has done wrong, he concludes, "Now my words have a purpose. They have the purpose, obviously, of silencing the laughter, of avoiding judgment personally, though there is apparently no escape. Is not the great thing that stands in the way of our escaping it the fact that we are the first to condemn ourselves?" He goes further than this, though, saying that overwhelmingly condemning himself gives him the right to judge others.

Women are more likely to use this technique than men. In most of the cultures of the world, women are socialized to give high priority to relationships. One part of caring for relationships is not bragging about oneself. It is part of feminine culture that approving of oneself is considered to be pride. A woman fears expressing that she is content with who she is for fear that others will react badly and accuse her of thinking that she is better than everyone else. These same women may also be given to gossip, however, protected by the fact that they have roundly criticized themselves first.

It would be wrong, though, to automatically conclude that any woman who operates within the "feminine culture" pattern of self-criticism is feeling a lot of shame. The cultural demands are strong, and self-criticism may just reflect a woman's fearing rejection from other women, rather than actually believing that she is deficient.

A variation on the weak defense is service. There are many motivations for serving our neighbors. It could be the result of loving the Lord and wanting to bless others. It could be a desire to have others think well of us. It could be a legally or culturally imposed obligation. It could have the purpose of making the helper feel good and virtuous afterward. It could be the fruit of low self-esteem, a product of shame.

Shame-prone people may use taking care of others as a way of generating acceptance and avoiding the rejection that they fear. Some get really involved in the problems and interests of others hoping to get rid of condemnation that they feel in themselves.

If I fear that others will reject me because I am not acceptable as a person, perhaps I can win them over by doing them favors. That way I make them indebted to me, whether economically, emotionally, or morally. It doesn't really matter to me that they have never asked for the favors I do for them, nor that they would really be happier if I didn't insist so much on imposing my services, nor even that they don't want done what I want to do. They have to accept me, they ought to love me, they should be grateful. If they don't love me as a result, they should be ashamed of themselves. And even if they never even acknowledge my work on their behalf—gratitude tends to be the most fragile of human virtues—I can still feel good inside because I have done what needed to be done. I am a good person. I don't owe anyone anything. I have attained moral superiority. I have stifled my own pain. But I have done it by shaming others.

In a relationship between helper and person being helped, it is obviously the helper who is superior and the person being helped who is deficient, needing help. Forcing someone to receive help shames him. It is very probable that those who have received my favors don't want to be in a position of owing me anything. I have just managed to pass my own shame to others. The helper has reduced the pain of shame at the expense of those helped.

I saw an incredible example of this one day when I went on a tourist excursion to an old mine with some older women. In order to enter one part of the mine we had to put on hard hats, and when we came back out and took off the helmets we all had "hat hair". Some of the ladies who usually got their hair done at the beauty parlor every week and always had lovely hair-dos looked really bedraggled. So one of the women got a comb and went around to each of the 15 or so others and told them she was going to fix their hair. In every case the offer was refused, but the helper wouldn't accept that. She insisted. In a couple of cases she tried to fix someone's hair by force, and was physically beaten off. Frustrated, she stomped off in a huff, muttering something about what did these people want, anyway. A little respect, maybe?

Camus has the narrator in *The Fall* describe how as a lawyer he manages to be superior to others by serving them. "I always obligated [my neighbor] without ever owing him anything. It set me above the judge, whom I judged in turn, above the defendant, whom I forced to gratitude." Later he remarks, "When I was concerned with others, I was so out of pure condescension, in utter freedom, and all the credit went to me: my self-esteem would go up a degree." This is how to serve one's self through the pretense of serving others.

This dynamic doesn't enrich relationships. It can leave those helped feeling ashamed and resentful. And besides, being busy about helping people doesn't really change your innermost feelings; it just buries the feelings a bit. You have to keep on working more and more in order to avoid feeling bad.

All this service and humility sounds so clean, so like the image of Christ, especially in contrast with the aggression of the strong cover-up. But it is very destructive both for the person who uses these tactics and for the people she uses them on. If you focus on your faults, talking a lot about them, it is possible that you might come to believe what you are saying. This can make you sad, especially if you find that other people don't contradict you like they are "supposed to". Women tend to suffer much more than men from depression, and it is very possible that the use of this way of dealing with shame may contribute to that problem.

This weak defense, if used with the same people for very long, may make them become tired of the manipulations. They may also feel shame and anger at having to receive constantly without being able to give anything in return. Two women both trying to serve and help the other without allowing any "payback" can end up being hostile to each other, both feeling the putdown of being served as shaming.

Questions for reflection:

1. Is what other people think of you important to you? What do you do or refrain from doing because you are afraid of what people will think?
2. Think of some incidents when you felt shame. How did you feel? What did you do as a result of how you felt? Think of

a time when you felt guilt. How did you feel? What did you do as a result of how you felt? From your own experience, what is the difference between guilt and shame?

3. Do you tend to experience more guilt or more shame in a difficult situation?

4. Can you see in your own life some of the characteristics of a shame-prone person? Think about some specific examples when you have acted like a person with a lot of shame. Is this an important attitude in your life?

5. When you feel shame do you prefer to defend yourself against the pain using the hard cover-up or the soft cover-up? Think of specific things that you do. Do you generally use just one technique or do you use sometimes one and sometimes the other? What results of your behaving in this way do you see in your own life and in the lives of the people around you?

CHAPTER **2** # Right from the Beginning

Adam and Eve

Shame is as old as humanity. It begins clear back when our first forefathers disobeyed God's commandment not to eat of the tree of the knowledge of good and evil.

> *When the woman saw that the fruit of the tree was good for food and pleasing to the eye, and also desirable for gaining wisdom, she took some and ate it. She also gave some to her husband, who was with her, and he ate it. Then the eyes of both of them were opened, and they realized they were naked; so they sewed fig leaves together and made coverings for themselves.*
>
> *Then the man and his wife heard the sound of the Lord God as he was walking in the garden in the cool of the day, and they hid from the Lord God among the trees of the garden. But the Lord God called to the man, "Where are you?"*

He answered, "I heard you in the garden, and I was afraid because I was naked; so I hid."

And he said "Who told you that you were naked? Have you eaten from the tree that I commanded you not to eat from?"

The man said, "The woman you put here with me—she gave me some fruit from the tree, and I ate it."

Then the Lord God said to the woman, "What is this you have done?"

The woman said, "The serpent deceived me, and I ate." . . .

The Lord God made garments of skin for Adam and his wife, and clothed them. (Genesis 3:6-13, 21).

Through Adam and Eve, sin entered into the world, and as a result we are all infected with it. We all sin. We all need a sacrifice that will take our guilt away. God himself made coverings of skins for Adam and Eve, and he dressed them. Some animal had to die to provide the skins, and this can be interpreted as the first sacrifice for guilt. God himself taught them that a sacrifice with blood was necessary to take away guilt.

But there is even more to it than that. I believe that when we read this passage with Western eyes in the 21st Century we miss something important. The first reaction of Adam and Eve after eating the fruit of the prohibited tree was to realize that they were naked and to try to hide themselves. First, they hid themselves from one another by making coverings out of fig leaves. Then they tried to hide from God.

They said they wanted to hide because they realized that they were naked. They were naked before, too, but it didn't bother them. Now it did. Before, they didn't have anything to hide. They accepted who they were and the limits that had been placed on them. But they wanted to be more than what they were. They wanted to be like God. They failed in the attempt. Now they knew that they had disobeyed, that they weren't what they should be. Far from being like God, they weren't even as like him as they used to be. They felt exposed. They wanted to disappear. They felt shame.

Because of their shame, their relationship with God was broken and they tried to hide from him. God didn't let them go without treating their condition, though. He searched them out and confronted them.

That was what they needed, but just the opposite of what they wanted. In their shame they didn't accept the guilt and responsibility for what they had done, but found someone else to blame. Adam blamed Eve (and indirectly blamed God for having given him the woman). Eve blamed the serpent.

God was not deceived. He did what he had to do in order to protect his creation and forced them out of the Garden. Even though Adam and Eve could not remain in the Garden, God provided for them. The sacrifice he made was not only to take away their guilt but also to cover their bodies, to cover their shame with clothing.

This is not to say that he took away their shame, because they were infected with what would come to be a typical characteristic of all humanity. Much later, when God would provide the definitive solution for guilt, he would also provide the solution for shame. Meanwhile, shame passed from them to their children, and then to us. Later we will examine how shame is passed from one person to another.

Cain

> Now Abel kept flocks, and Cain worked the soil. In the course of time Cain brought some of the fruits of the soil as an offering to the Lord. But Abel brought fat portions from some of the firstborn of his flock. The Lord looked with favor on Abel and his offering, but on Cain and his offering he did not look with favor. So Cain was very angry, and his face was downcast.
> Then the Lord said to Cain, "Why are you angry? Why is your face downcast? If you do what is right, will you not be accepted? But if you do not do what is right, sin is crouching at your door; it desires to have you, but you must master it." (Genesis 4:2b–7)

Better authors than I have dedicated whole books to exploring the mentality of Cain and the relationship between him and his brother Abel. Here I will limit myself to making explicit what is normally assumed as understood but which is seldom developed: the role shame plays in this story.

We don't have many details about the lives of these sons of Adam and Eve. We just know that one day the two of them came to offer something to the Lord. The Lord accepted the younger brother and his offering but did not accept the elder brother and his offering. There is a lot of theological speculation about the motive for the difference, usually focusing on the fact that Abel had brought an offering of blood and Cain one of vegetables. Much later God would prescribe offerings of grain and wine also, together with the blood offerings.

Hebrews 11:4 says that by faith Abel offered a better sacrifice than Cain did and by faith he was commended as a righteous man, when God spoke well of his offerings. The truth is that we don't really know why God accepted one and rejected the other, nor how God communicated to them his acceptance or rejection.

But we do know that God paid more attention to the individuals who presented the offerings than he did to the offerings themselves. The person is mentioned before the offering. He looked with favor on Abel and his offering, but on Cain and his offering he did not look with favor.

This made Cain angry. He was actually furious. He suffered public humiliation when God obviously received his little brother and his offering in preference to Cain and his. As the elder brother, Cain was accustomed to receiving the honor of his position. Both brothers had brought something from their own lives as an offering, and it was inconceivable that his was not the best. Besides, in order to get an animal for a blood sacrifice it is possible that he would have had to negotiate with Abel, to buy one from his flocks. Shame attacked.

He was furious, but with whom? Fury is not necessarily directed at the one who has caused the shame. It can explode at anyone. Cain himself was the responsible one, but he didn't want to be angry with himself and admit his guilt. Cain deserved the shame that he was feeling. Now he would have to choose a response. He could receive God's correction, confess his error, change his attitude and behavior and receive forgiveness, or he could blame someone else for what was wrong.

"Obviously" it was God himself who had done the damage by making Cain's fault evident. Many centuries later someone would write a proverb saying, "A man's own folly ruins his life, yet his heart rages against the Lord." (Proverbs 19:3)

He could get angry with God (a lot of people do), but the great difference in power between the two of them made it impossible to argue with God and come out being right. But look; Abel also had part of the blame. If Abel had not made his acceptable offering at the same time, Cain's failure would not have been so noticeable. It was easy to express his anger toward Abel.

God spoke to him immediately about his attitude. Note that his intimacy with God had not been broken. God was speaking to him and he could perceive it and respond. God did not reproach him for having offered a wrong sacrifice, but rather for the expression on his face, which clearly showed his anger. God was trying to help him learn right behavior. This was only the second generation since creation, and they didn't have a long history from which Cain could have learned. Patiently and directly God spoke to him to correct his error. If the problem could be solved, there would be no long-term consequences.

God said that there was no reason for so much emotion, since all he had to do to be accepted was behave well. With strong anger, there was danger. Sin was at the door waiting for him. The last phrase of God's warning, "it desires to have you, but you must master it," is also a warning for us. Sin wanted to have power over Cain but he could and should overcome it. Our enemy also wants to master us, as is explained in I Peter 5:8, our enemy the devil prowls around like a roaring lion looking for someone to devour. The following phrase in I Peter says, "Resist him." This is what God told Cain, too. Sin wanted to swallow him up, but he needed to resist. This was not outside his power. God even promised him that if he fought the temptation he would win!

In the end Cain did not resist temptation. He killed his brother. The attack may have been a complete surprise for Abel, who may not have suspected what was brewing in the heart of his brother. Abel had done nothing to provoke the assault, at least not on purpose. He accepted the invitation to go out into the fields.

Since up to this point no human had died, it is possible that Cain himself did not know for sure what would be the result of his actions, but he could have suspected from having observed the death of animals. In his fury, he became the first murderer.

He gave God His blood sacrifice! If his original fault had been not offering a blood sacrifice, as some theologians affirm, he had now corrected the problem, offering the blood of Abel. But such twisting the commandments of God is not admissible. God heard the blood of Abel which called out from the earth, demanding justice. Once more he spoke with Cain. This time the punishment was permanent and Cain became separated from God and from others. The separation that his parents had experienced was repeated as a result of his shame.

God put a mark on Cain to protect him in case anyone wanted to kill him for what he had done. But the very protecting mark was at the same time a mark of shame. He would never again be able to mix with others without everyone knowing his crime. He became isolated.

So often the "sacrifice" we make in order to get rid of our shame, especially deserved shame, hurts or destroys our neighbors. Envy, a common result of shame, destroys the life of those who practice it, and also the lives of their neighbors who have something better, something desired but not achieved by the envier. Nevertheless, the inheritance that Cain passes on is not so much envy, nor betrayal, nor furious murder. It is shame, the profound sense that makes a person feel inferior and unacceptable. It doesn't have to be that way now. In Christ, God has given us a sacrifice which speaks better things than the condemnation spoken by the blood of Abel (Hebrews 12:24).

Questions for reflection:

1. Contrast the histories of Adam, Eve and Cain to see the variety of ways in which guilt and shame are manifested. How did each respond to shame? Did they use the hard or soft cover-up? How did they respond when God reproached them? How did they turn out in the end as far as their guilt and shame were concerned?

2. How do you respond when God reproaches you for something? How do you respond when another human being reproaches you? Does it make any difference in your response if the other person is right or not? In general, what

is the result of this in your life? What is the result of your pattern of reacting in the lives of those who live near you?

3. We can suppose that Adam and Eve did not start life with a load of shame, but rather that they started to experience it after they disobeyed. Nevertheless the actions of Cain make one suspect that when he went to offer the sacrifice he already had a load of shame in his heart. In what sense was it harder for him to obey God than it would have been if he hadn't had the load of shame? Do you have a load of shame that makes it difficult to consistently love your neighbor?

CHAPTER 3 This Stuff Is Contagious

My mother grew up in a disadvantaged neighborhood. Nobody actually said that Cedar City was on the "wrong side of the river", but everyone knew it. My father's family, though, lived on the right side. When they were married, my mother struggled to prove to her in-laws that she was worthy to associate with them. She stopped visiting her own family, and we only celebrated holidays with my father's family. Even today I have no idea how her family celebrated Christmas, New Year's, Easter, or birthdays. I'm not even sure of all of the names of my first cousins on my mother's side. Mom worked hard to get out of Cedar City and to shake the shame of being "inferior".

One effective way to get out of Cedar City was a good education. She was the only university graduate in her large family, and later she went back to get a master's degree. When I was a teenager she got a job as principal of a school. When money started to come in from her work, she drew up plans for a new house, a big brick house on a corner lot with as many of the latest gadgets as possible. But this wasn't enough. Every three years or so she remodeled. The house kept getting bigger and more impressive as the family got smaller when my brother and I left to go to school. My mother never admitted publicly where she was from until after all of the members of my father's family had died without having children. A few years before she died, she wrote a history of Cedar City for the historical society.

One could say that my mother got out of Cedar City, but she could never get Cedar City out of herself. She was always worried about what others might think of her, but in spite of her study and work she never managed to make herself into the acceptable person she wanted to be. She accumulated nice things and was the first in the neighborhood to get the latest gadgets. When she died, we found literally dozens of sets of china and elegant crystal, some of them trimmed with gold and platinum, few of which she had ever used. The only visitors that had ever come to the house were a few members of my father's family, once a year for New Year's dinner. We weren't worthy.

I drank in this way of thinking with my milk.

When I was young we didn't have a lot of money and there were a lot of things we just couldn't have. I went to school in home-sewn clothes and hand-me-downs instead of the pretty clothes that my classmates had. We didn't have a car and we had to drag groceries home from town a mile away in my brother's toy wagon. "Everybody knew" we were second class.

Reluctantly I accepted the belief that we were somehow defective, and this affected my opinions about everything. For example in school we learned that at noon the sun was directly overhead. In my yard, though, I could see clearly that the sun was not overhead, but far to the south. In a whole year it never got to be overhead. In winter, it never even got close. Instead of realizing that since we lived in the north it had to be like that, I came to the conclusion that the sun over my house wasn't as good as the sun elsewhere. I always gave the "right" answer when asked about it on a test, but it wasn't until much later that I realized what an indication this was of my deep sense of inferiority.

For me, too, studying seemed to be the best way to climb the ladder of acceptability. My parents pushed me to excel in school. They always said that grades weren't important, that they only wanted me to do my best. But it soon became clear that any grade except an "A" was a sign

31

that I was doing less than my best. With each hard-earned report card I got reprieve until next time.

I kept trying to please them in high school and college, but in graduate school it was getting harder to come out on top, since the curve had caught up with me. When I announced that I was quitting my doctoral program in chemistry to get married, they had a hard time concealing their disappointment. Never again did I experience their acceptance. I had betrayed their hope that I would make the family worthy, and there was no forgiveness.

When my kids were older, I went back to school and finally got my doctorate, but in psychology. Even this wasn't enough to earn my way back into my family's good graces.

I didn't reason any of this out at the time. I just reproduced in my own life what my mother had done with hers.

Parents are powerful models. Children imitate what they do. Children observe the emotional style of their mothers or fathers and come to the conclusion (probably without having thought it through in words) that that is the correct way to handle situations. If a girl repeatedly sees her mother react with shame, she may learn to imitate a pattern of physical shrinking back, diverted gaze and declarations of lack of personal worth. If a boy observes that his father reacts to frustration with anger, he may develop a pattern of anger in his life, too. Cain may have learned from his parents that the best way to deal with having done something wrong was to blame someone else.

Shame is transmitted from one generation to another in a family.

My children once gave me a lapel button that read, "Insanity is hereditary. You get it from your kids." Well . . . no. Shame, on the other hand *is* contagious. We get it from others, especially from other family members. A person heavily burdened with shame can infect others. In this way having something to hide has come to be a part of the human condition.

Generally speaking, children are not born with guilt or shame. Shame comes when they are old enough to distinguish themselves as beings separate from others and to differentiate between situations. The sense of shame is developed over many years and the process continues for a lifetime.

Dr. Charles Kraft, author of *Two Hours to Freedom* and veteran of more than 25 years of experience in helping people find freedom from shame describes a possible exception to this generalization. He says in a personal note, "My experience, both counseling and personally, is that shame often develops in the womb. When a person comes and (like me) his/her parents were not married when he/she was conceived, I've often found a high level of shame. My parents weren't married and I didn't know it till I was about 50. So I lived with shame and self hatred for about 50 years related, I believe, to my conception. My brothers and sister experienced my father much differently than I did with no such shame but I was ashamed to be alive. In counseling, then, if the person tells me he/she was conceived before marriage, I look for shame and it's usually there." This shame could come from being treated in a shaming way by the parents, of course, but this other possibility needs to be taken into account.

We acquire both deserved and undeserved shame from other people, especially from our parents. We are taught which ways of acting are acceptable in our culture and which are not. If we go beyond the limits society imposes, people disapprove, and we feel their rejection. In this way they teach us to wear clothes, bathe, tell the truth, and not steal, although the result does depend on who is doing the teaching and what kind of example they give. We learn habits of conduct as a way of avoiding the pain of shame.

An important source of shame in families is poor management of anger. The Biblical standard is that we are to lay aside falsehood and speak the truth with one another. We may become angry but must resolve the matter the same day so as not to give the devil an opportunity. (Ephesians 4:25-27) There are two reasons for not allowing grievances to pile up. One is that they tend to become set in our minds. If we let it sit overnight, we wake up with it in the morning. If we let it go for several days or let the instances pile up, our anger increases and it is harder to deal with the matter objectively.

The other reason for dealing with this right off is that with one instance of a problem we can say we don't like such and such a behavior on the part of someone else. This is a complaint, but it is not against the person. It attributes guilt, but not shame. If we allow the behavior to continue before we complain, it becomes harder to deal with it as an isolated incident, and we complain about a habit or, worse, a character flaw in the other person. This is criticizing the person, and is shaming of the other person. If the process goes on for a long time before we complain, and the resentment builds up, character flaws are called out in disrespectful terms and the person is definitely shamed. The possibility of correcting the situation amicably becomes vanishingly small and the other person may be flooded with hurt. Calling the other person nasty names is so hurtful that Jesus says that this behavior is comparable to murder and may be punishable by the hell of fire (Matthew 5:21-22).

It is more or less simple to avoid being shamed for certain specific conducts. You just have to obey the rules. But what happens if the rules aren't very clear or very fair? Or if you just don't understand why they yell at you and say you are an idiot? Or if you somehow end up being wrong no matter what you do?

Sad to say, there are no perfect parents because we are all sinners. We all have hurts from wounds we got in childhood, and when we get to be parents we all hurt our children. We all have to live with the wounds somehow, but some people have received more undeserved shame than others. Parents can deeply hurt their children when they transmit messages such as "you are bad," "you aren't able to do that," "you will never amount to anything," "you are useless," and other variations on the theme.

The emotional environment in which you live as a child will also help form your future emotional style. The psychiatrist Michael Lewis claims that if as a child you were just together with a shame-prone parent this will have produced the same tendency to be shame-prone in your own life. He claims that an environment with a lot of shame is automatically full of stress, and when children are under a lot of stress, they tend to blame themselves for whatever happens.

If Mommy and Daddy are shaming each other, the child will actually assume that he or she is responsible for that, even though an outsider would know that the child is not at fault. If a child continues to live in an environment like that, he will probably suffer from chronic shame. The psychologist Joan Pulakos has shown that children who come from dysfunctional families have more shame as adults.

In his studies on the dynamics of families, John Bradshaw found that the tendency to feel shame is transmitted by means of the rules that dysfunctional families impose on themselves. There are six basic rules that each member of a dysfunctional family must obey. These rules are not exclusive to dysfunctional families, and they are destructive wherever they are strongly enforced.

The first rule is control. Control is an important protection against shame. If I can control what everyone else says and does, I can guarantee that they will not shame me. If the parents try to control the actions of each person, all of the interactions between members of the family, their own emotions and those of everyone else, too, the children will soon learn that everything that they feel, think, do and say is subject to the judgment and control of others. They learn to keep constant vigil over themselves so as to stay out of trouble, and they learn to want to control others.

The second rule is perfectionism. If I always behave myself and I am always right, I am not in too much danger of being shamed. Family members in a dysfunctional family live with an imposed image, something they have to live up to. Errors, accidents and sins are not permitted. If anyone fails, they cover up what they have done in order to avoid the condemnation of everyone else. Nobody is truly perfect, of course, so they all live in a dangerous environment. Someone might find out that they aren't as good as the rest of the family wants to pretend they are.

The third rule is blaming. Any time anything bad happens, someone has to be to blame for it. There is no such thing as no-fault insurance. Depending on each person's style, whether they choose the soft or hard protection against shame, they might blame someone else or themselves. Their family, the only people in the world who could truly support and affirm them, are programmed to look for their faults and shame them whenever possible.

The fourth rule is not to trust anyone. In a dysfunctional family, promises are not kept. Your family can betray you. There is no respect and no loyalty.

The fifth rule is that individuals are not permitted the liberty of perceiving things as they really do perceive them. You may not imagine for yourself, or think or interpret ideas in your own way. You must not want and choose what you really desire. As a result, it may actually be more comfortable not to feel anything at all, since your feelings are also up for criticism. These things are decided ahead of time in shame-filled families. If you have an opinion or something you like that does not correspond to what has been determined, you are bad. Everyone has to be of the same political party, support the same football team and like the same kind of music.

There is a drawing by the Argentinian cartoonist Joaquín Salvador Lavado (Quino) which shows a child and his parents in their house. The whole house is decorated with squares, from the furniture and the wallpaper to the clothes people wear. On the floor is a paper with a drawing, obviously made by the child, which shows a spiral. The parents are looking at the boy with condemnation. The boy's head is down, his eyes fixed on the floor. He has violated the rule of being a square.

Even in a healthy family, the child who is different from his parents may suffer more. There aren't many parents who take a lot of trouble to understand well a child who is different from them. The athlete in a family of musicians, the artist in a family of scientists, the dedicated student in a business-oriented family, the actor in a family of educators, will have to struggle so that family members will understand and accept them. In a dysfunctional family any child who is different is shamed.

I can testify personally to the power of this rule. The rules about likes and opinions were very strong as I was growing up. There was an official family opinion about TV shows, food, music, dress, acceptable after-school activities, sports, you-name-it, and if anyone ventured an alternate opinion it was considered almost a moral fault. When at 12 years old I wanted to start shaving my legs; they forbid me to do it, saying that only bad girls did that. One day when I was an adult and in graduate school my mother found out I liked yogurt. She acted as though I had personally offended her. How could a daughter of hers have fallen so low? I waited until I was married with three children of my own to work up the nerve to have my ears pierced, since this was something that was Not Done. Even then I had to struggle against the sensation of being a loose woman.

Growing up, I could form opinions by collecting data and using reasoning, but likes and dislikes come from within. Obviously what was inside was unacceptable to my family, and what is on the inside is the important part of me. Even now as an adult I frequently find out what other people like before deciding if I will let them know what I like (if indeed I even know what I like after deferring to others' tastes for so many years). I am always surprised when someone else actually likes what I like. Even though I know exactly where this problem comes from, I still can't believe I have good taste about anything.

The sixth rule is silence. If anything goes wrong, you mustn't talk about it, whether to a family member or to an outsider. If we don't talk about how Daddy hits Mommy, or that Suzy is always angry, or that Mary cries a lot, or that Uncle Joe drinks too much, there is no problem. It is like having a rhinoceros in the living room, but everyone acts like it isn't there. And more than anything else, one mustn't talk about the rules. Most of the power of the rules comes from the fact that officially they don't exist.

Nobody talked about the rules in my family. I really began to notice them when I visited my parents' house after I was married, accompanied by my children. Since we lived in another country, we didn't visit very much. I knew the rules of the house, even though I was unaware of them as rules because we had never talked about them. But my children had not been brought up with those rules, and they began to act freely. Of course the grandparents were offended many times a day. Sometimes when the matter was really problematic I tried to explain to the kids that such and such a thing wasn't done in Grandma and Grandpa's house, but mostly I was too tired of the rules to want to perpetuate them. In the end I just let them ignore the rules. Later it became evident that my parents preferred my brother's daughter, who lived closer, visited more often, and learned and obeyed the rules.

Attitudes count

What parents say to children when they are rebuking the child for something can be especially damaging. Ideally, the parent corrects what the children have done without attacking the children. But in the heat of the moment the children are often shamed.

Even if parents don't say or do anything noticeably hostile or hurtful, just denying the child love makes the child feel like a total failure as a person. If parents do not express love to their child, the child will probably feel not only unloved but unworthy of love.

The psychologist Ronald Rohner has received many honors for his more than 2,000 studies in different cultures all over the world, in which he examines the effect on children of whether their parents accept and affirm them or reject them. In all the cultures he studied, children suffer deep long-term damage when they believe that their parents reject them. It doesn't seem to matter whether an outsider looking at the situation thinks there has been rejection, or whether the parents really do reject the child. Both the parents and the outsider might say that nothing hurtful is happening, but the child may still perceive that there is rejection. The only thing that matters to the child's mental health is how the child interprets the situation.

Children in every culture in the world need the acceptance of their parents and of other important people. Rohner had children describe their own characteristics; then he looked at how their classification correlated with whether they thought their parents rejected them. If they felt themselves rejected, they categorized themselves as hostile and aggressive, either dependent or super independent, having low self-esteem, inadequate, emotionally unresponsive, and having a negative view of the world. They get depressed and are more likely to abuse alcohol or drugs. They have been shamed, and they develop the tendency to feel shame habitually.

Rohner has found three ways in which parents' actions affect their children. Of course their actions are based mostly on how they feel toward the child. When parents feel *affection* for their children, they show it. If they feel *hostile*, that shows up as aggressiveness. When they feel *indifferent*, they push the child aside and don't give him the attention he needs. Sometimes the child feels rejection from the parents, even though neither the parents nor an impartial outside observer can detect anything specific which could cause the feeling.

Here we don't need to list specific things that can produce a feeling of rejection, but rather bring out the importance of the *child's perception* of his relation with his parents. If the child knows that he is loved and appreciated, he can develop as a person with confidence and a positive concept of himself and his role in the world. But if he thinks that his parents do not accept him, almost always he concludes that the reason for this sad situation is that he is not acceptable.

Both children and adults tend to think of themselves what they believe other people who are important to them might think. So if they see that the people closest to them do not love them, they conclude that they don't inspire love and that they are probably unworthy of being loved. Knowing that one is unacceptable and unworthy of love produces shame.

The psychologist John Gottman has rigorously studied what happens when children make bids for their parents' attention. A bid may be anything the child does or says to get attention, such as bringing something to show, wanting a book read, asking a question, pulling on Mommy's clothing, crying, knocking baby brother down, or doing something exceptional. The kind of response that he usually receives has great consequences.

If the parents usually give the attention he wants when he makes a bid for it, the child learns that he is accepted and loved. If the answer is usually harsh, hostile or aggressive, the child tends to respond with anger, rejecting strongly the person to whom he was trying to relate. Over time and with a lot of repetitions of the hostile treatment, the anger may build up to a point where the relationship is permanently damaged. However, if the answer is indifference or lack of interest, the child does not respond with anger, but with collapse.

Gottman describes how he has watched many children who receive indifference to their bids for attention. Their shoulders and head fall like a deflated balloon. They give up. It was possibly not the parent's intention to reject or discourage the child. Perhaps they were just absorbed in their own problems to the point where each interaction with their child consisted in telling them to be quiet or go away. Children look to their parents to validate and direct their feelings. When parents respond with indifference, the children start to doubt themselves. They may ask themselves, "What is the matter with me that I feel so bad?"

It seems surprising that indifference could damage someone more than direct hostility, but I can testify personally that it is true. One of my happiest memories from my high school years is having overheard a group of five or six other students criticizing me. I wasn't deliberately eavesdropping on them, but I had come to where they were, looking for something, and heard them accidentally. They said I was stuck up and self-centered and thought I was better than everybody else. What they were saying was at least partially true, since I was definitely self-centered, but they didn't know how inferior I felt. When I left after a few minutes, I was practically dancing for joy. I had discovered that I was so important that people remembered that I existed even when I wasn't present. People weren't indifferent to me! I was somebody! They actually thought enough of me that they wasted their time gossiping about me!

Maybe the harshest way in which a parent can shame a child is by sexual abuse. This is more than just physical abuse, in most cases of a girl. It is also an attack on her most intimate being, a total lack of respect. Normally the girl is taught that she herself is to blame for what the abuser has done. The girl who is sexually abused needs to know that she is still a valuable, acceptable, and loved person, in spite of the false guilt and the shame which she feels. But unless someone helps her and convinces her of this good news, she will probably not change her perception of herself as damaged goods.

Some children are more susceptible to negative messages than others are. Negative messages that are often repeated will get inside the child's thoughts and be repeated over and over. They become an interior voice that is always chattering on in their heads. A recording of what Mommy and Daddy said or a description of what they did will be constantly playing in their thoughts. Even when Mommy and Daddy didn't actually say or do that, if the child thinks they did, it is just as bad. And even when those who made the negative comments are no longer around, even when they are dead, the perceived messages continue to control thoughts and emotions.

The influence of society

The messages don't necessarily have to come from parents. School teachers, who serve as substitute parents during many hours of the week, can have a strong influence. Studies have shown that teachers who expect much of students and make it clear that they respect them find that their expectations are met. But teachers who insult the children or look down on them not only make the child uncomfortable for a while but also may inspire years of doubt about their abilities and acceptability. And if poor treatment by a teacher is accompanied by the cruelty that children traditionally practice on one another, many people can come out of school having learned mostly that they themselves are shameful.

All over the world there is prejudice against girls, even today. And all over the world the prevalence of depression among women reflects this rejection and the shame that goes with it. Boys also receive negative messages from society. A common one is that boys shouldn't cry because only girls cry, when of course crying is something that all of humanity has in common. The tacit implication, of course, is that the boy won't want to act like a girl. This negative message is very economical, because while it shames the boy for having cried, at the same time it shames his sister for being a girl. Two for the price of one.

People of minority racial groups have to put up with lots of negative messages. We are shamed when our ethnic group is looked down on by another group.

I never appreciated how harsh the discrimination that Blacks, Hispanics, Chinese, and other ethnic groups must feel, until I went to Grand Rapids, Michigan, and found a much milder discrimination directed toward me. There I saw billboards proclaiming "If you ain't Dutch, you ain't much". I have no problem with the Dutch celebrating their ancestry and culture, but I wish they could do it without insulting me. And that was just a billboard. I could look at it and leave it behind instead of living with it all the time. It didn't have anything to do with my having to sit in the back of the bus or get a smaller paycheck or live in a poor part of town. Anyone trying to find out how a minority person feels needs to take the shame factor into account.

One of the more difficult families I have tried to help was a Mexican father and mother, who had immigrated to the U.S. ten years before with their three children. The parents had been slow to learn English, and actually the father refused to learn it. The teen-age daughter was thoroughly acculturated to Anglo Los Angeles, and felt shame because of her father's insistence on keeping his rural Mexican ways. He felt shame because his daughter was acting in ways he would never have permitted in Mexico. He refused to speak even the English he knew; she refused to admit that she even understood Spanish, though she obviously did. The pleas of the mother and the other two children were not enough to soften the stance of either, and eventually shame drove the daughter out of the family.

Being poorer than one's schoolmates, being gay, having a physical or mental disability, not knowing how to manage social situations well, or any other difference that might make one stand out negatively, invites nasty comments and cruel jokes that stick in the memory and the soul of the child for his whole life. If the messages keep coming, the person may begin to believe them and repeat them in his or her head. They also become the interior voice that influences self-image. In an extreme case the messages may lead to total rebellion against the shaming system, and maybe even to violence.

It is in context of this shaming that we need to understand "gay pride", "black is beautiful" and other attempts to change the thinking, not necessarily of the people who are on the outside of the movement but rather of those for whom the put-downs have been crippling.

Some children have better situations than others. I did some research in some evangelical churches in the south of Spain, and also in the United States. Some of the people had been born into families which were part of the church and had been brought up in faith. Others had come to faith through outside influences, usually as adults or teenagers. I asked the people to fill out a questionnaire about the way their parents had brought them up and about the presence of shame in their lives. They all had in common that they were part of a Christian community at the time of filling out the questionnaire.

About their upbringing, I asked especially if they had felt affirmed and accepted, rejected, or treated with indifference by their parents.

The characteristics of shame asked about for the most part did not sound negative. For instance, I asked if they had very high standards for themselves and felt bad if they didn't live up to them, if they had trouble forgiving themselves, if they liked themselves, if they liked to help people but were upset when others didn't want their help, if they feared being considered ridiculous, and if there were things they wouldn't do because of being afraid of what "they" would say.

I found that children who were born and brought up in believing households reported significantly more love and affirmation from their parents and later felt significantly less shame than children who were raised in non-believing households and who became believers later.

This advantage was lost, however, if the church that the family attended taught that nobody should think well of themselves because that would be pride. It seems that in the desire to keep children humble it is possible to go too far and teach them that they are nothing, thus denying them appreciation for the good qualities they have.

Contrary to popular "wisdom", time does not take away the pain of shame. Sometimes it even magnifies the pain, if we meditate on how people have hurt us. Adults continue to have the same negative internal messages that were recorded when they were children.

Once I was giving a course in Christian counseling to a group of pastors. As an illustration of how negative messages can be transmitted, I imitated as best I could an angry mother yelling at her child. I included all of the insults I had heard mothers heap on their children. That had an effect that I had not anticipated. We had to stop the class because half the pastors were crying. The pain of receiving those phrases from their mothers was still fresh.

When we have been rejected and unjustly shamed, we can feel rejected even when nobody is rejecting us. This provokes self rejection and shows up as low self-esteem, perhaps with anger toward those who have rejected us, fear that it might happen again, and even hatred. Our spiritual enemy takes advantage of us to augment our pain and do us even more damage.

Shame is contagious. It propagates by itself. Shamed people shame other people. If someone feels the pain of shame, somehow they can get some relief if they pass on to others the insult or the indifference that hurt them. If they believe that they are useless, they can tell someone else that they are worse than useless, and for the moment they are better than the other person at least. Of course it doesn't really make them feel good, but at least the pain is shared. The result is that this hurts the other person, probably reinforcing whatever feeling of shame he may have acquired from other hurts. Later that person also will have the temptation to shame a third person, who will do the same with someone else. There is a famous sequence where the boss fights with his wife in the morning, which leads to his reaming out an employee, who goes home at night and yells at his wife, who spanks a child for a minimal offense, after which the child hits a smaller sibling, who goes and kicks the dog. That is about the way it works, though it doesn't always happen so quickly in one day.

In this way a whole family can quickly become shamed. Later the shame can spread to the whole neighborhood, school, and place of work. The whole city, and even the whole society can be affected. Even though individuals may have had fantastic parents, the society can make sure they get shamed: the neighbor, the mail carrier, the bureaucrat behind the grill of a government office. Just one shame-prone person is enough to infect a whole country.

So once a community has been infected with the virus of shame, all of the members of the community are vulnerable to being shamed as they reject one another.

The process could be well summarized by something a Costa Rican fruit seller once told me. She said that bananas are like people. If you knock them about a lot they will go bad.

Criticizing other people is a temptation for shame-prone individuals, because it serves to take away attention from their own faults and focus the attention on those of other people. Especially if someone else can be blamed for what the blamer has done, it will relieve the pain a bit. We all have the tendency to criticize others for being and doing what we ourselves are and do. Someone has rightly said that if we want to know what our own faults are, we should think of people we don't like, and figure out why we don't like them. It is very possible that we have the same faults that we don't like in others.

When we criticize someone publicly we may do more than just shame them. We can destroy them. Sometimes the criticism is said in a joking sort of way, but this does not prevent the hurt. Teasing may hurt even more than open hostility, because the person being teased is supposed to think it is funny.

Judging others is a very dangerous activity. In our attempts to defend ourselves we can open the door to receiving in return the same sort of treatment. Jesus said that we should not judge others so that we would not be judged (Matthew 7:1-5). God could judge us like that because he knows us completely. But most likely the verse refers to the fact that other people will give back to us the treatment we give them. We need to cleanse ourselves first, and above all get rid of the shame that inspires us to criticize and hurt others. Those who gossip and run down others should take special note.

King David recognizes the hurtfulness of these things when he says in Psalm 101:5, "Whoever slanders his neighbor in secret, him will I put to silence; whoever has haughty eyes and a proud heart, him will I not endure." Some translations say "destroys" instead of "slanders", but in a larger sense slandering is destroying. Silencing the gossip limits a little bit the propagation of shame and helps others to avoid following the bad example. The temptation, of course, is to speak badly of those who speak badly, and continue the process.

We tend to think of our shame as our own, personal, private thing, but it isn't. While we live with anger, fear, and hatred, either we condemn others or we try to control them, and we are propagating rejection and shame in those around us. With our reaction to our own shame and with our attempts to protect ourselves, we shame others and infect our family, friends, neighbors, and coworkers. If we feel shame because someone has shamed us in the past and we defend ourselves by being the first to attack others (rejecting them before they can reject us), and if we offend them, they get discouraged (at least). If they also have a tendency to feel shame, this may provoke them to defend themselves by shaming someone else.

Jesus talks about this in the Sermon on the Mount. In Matthew 5:22 we read, "But I tell you that anyone who is angry with his brother will be subject to judgment. Again, anyone who says to his brother, 'Raca' (an Aramaic term of contempt) is answerable to the Sanhedrin. But anyone who says, 'You fool!' will be in danger of the fire of hell." Why does he call out such terrible consequences for an offense as small as a little insult? Insults which may seem common and without importance ("don't you even know how to take a joke?") can destroy people.

Questions for reflection:

1. How did your parents manage their own experiences of shame? Have they been models for you? In what ways do you act like they did? If you act differently, has this been a decision you made deliberately, or is it due to other influences? If you are a parent, what examples are you giving to your children?

2. Did any of the rules of dysfunctional families govern your family of origin? What was the effect of the rules on the life of the family? What lasting effect have they had on your own life? Do you still obey the rules? If you are a parent, do you employ the same or different rules in your present family?

3. How did your parents react to your bids for attention? Were you accepted, rejected, or treated with indifference? Were there chronic negative messages in their way of treating you and talking with you? What has been the result in your life of the direct treatment that you received from them? If you are a parent, do you treat your children like your parents treated you?

4. Were there people or situations in the society at large that shamed you when you were a child? What has been the long-term effect of this shaming on you? In the environment where you live now are there elements that regularly shame people?

5. Among the people with whom you associate now is it common to hear criticisms or gossip? What do you do when you hear people gossiping?

6. How do you react to someone who apparently uses the strong way of covering up his shame? How does this affect your relationship with that person? How do you react to someone who uses the soft defense? What are the results of your reactions on this relationship? Which is your preferred style? How can you avoid propagating shame when you need to confront people of your same style or the opposite style?

CHAPTER 4 Spiritual
Aspects
of Shame

It is easy to see that our emotional and physical states are related. If I have a headache I may become less patient with others or with circumstances. A lot of anxiety may make my stomach hurt, or may make me lose sleep at night so I am constantly tired. Feeling depressed can even lower my resistance to disease.

The relationship between our emotional and spiritual states is less obvious, though, possibly because we are not accustomed to observing that. People who are accustomed to daily prayer know that being in the midst of an emotional dispute with someone can affect their ability to pray. Conversely, not being up-to-date in my prayer life may make it all too easy to enter into disputes. Since all of the parts of us are linked together, it is not surprising that our emotions affect our spiritual well-being, nor that our spiritual life affects our emotional life. Shame may have spiritual effects, and also spiritual roots.

Lack of love

Jesus commanded us to love one another. Loving other Christians is an important way of showing our love for Jesus (John 15:10-14, I John 3:14-16). In I John 4:8 we even find that someone who does not love does not know God, since God is love. Some people have suggested that being self-centered is the basic cause of a lack of love, and even that it is the essence of sin.

A person who has love is described in I Corinthians 13:4-7: "Love is patient, love is kind. It does not envy, it does not boast, it is not proud. It is not rude, it is not self-seeking, it is not easily angered, it keeps no record of wrongs. Love does not delight in evil but rejoices with the truth. It always protects, always trusts, always hopes, always perseveres."

The effect that shame has on a person is in many ways the opposite of love. Shame causes us to become self-centered, often impatient and putting up with others' faults. Being self-centered we will not be motivated to be kind, unless we are using the soft method of dealing with our shame and want to use others in order to feel good or manipulate them to get something. A shame-prone person is prone to envy. If he is using the strong defense against shame, he enjoys boasting. He is more comfortable with the bad things that happen to others than the good things, and, as we will see, is even proud. So the habit of feeling shame is an important barrier to the love we are supposed to have for others.

Jesus said that the way the world would know that we were his disciples was by noticing that we love one another. "A new command I give you: Love one another. As I have loved you, so you must love one another. By this all men will know that you are my disciples, if you love one another." (John 13:34-35). If we can't shake off our fears enough to love our brothers and our neighbors from the heart, not only will our fellowship in the church be shallow, but we will put a stumbling block in the way of the unbelievers around us.

I was originally attracted to the group of Christian students through whom I eventually came to know Christ by the way they treated one another. They appreciated one another, they helped each other, they were concerned when another had problems.

They even cared about me. This was such a different attitude from what I had found in other contexts that it got my attention. It seemed that they didn't even see the little sign I must have had on my forehead which said that I was unworthy of attention. They weren't ashamed to be seen in public with me. They applauded my successes. They prayed when I had needs. Even though they didn't seem very impressed with the achievements I used to gain the respect of other people, that didn't bother me much. They even defended me when they heard negative gossip about me! They had to put up with a lot of garbage from me, since I had never had any friends before and I didn't know how to treat them. But the result was that they loved me enough that I came to know the Lord.

I enjoyed this love for a couple of years as I grew in my faith. I believed that all Christians must be like the ones I knew. It was a horrible shock to me to discover the reality of the lives of others who said they were Christ-followers. When I heard them running each other down, saw them fighting over details, lying, and discouraging one another, I began to wonder if they really had Jesus in their lives. God had given me a specially protected environment for a while. It was what I needed to get going. How wonderful if everyone could live like that! How effective our efforts at evangelism would be if we could introduce people to such love!

Sadly not all Christian groups are like that. Infighting, jockeying for position and power, and control issues often are a result of some people's shame getting out of control. Instead of "in love preferring one another" (Philippians 2:3) we are actually capable of fighting over who gets to lead the women's society, who participates in the public worship, or who controls the purse strings. Have you ever heard of anyone fighting over who will be allowed the privilege of cleaning the restrooms? A lot of this infighting is a result of individuals who have been shamed and are protecting themselves. We'll look at this some more later.

Gossip is a major motivating force in many churches. It seems so genteel, so holy, that it even happens publicly in prayer meetings, as people ask for prayer for so-and-so who has done this-and-that. But even with this trapping of supposed concern for the brother or sister (never someone who is present), it is usually nothing better than defamation of character.

The apostle Paul writing in Romans 1:29-32 puts gossip in the same list as murder, and says that people who do it are worthy of death. Destroying someone's good name, even with the admonition to pray for them, is still destruction of the person. It is still putting someone down in order for the speaker and the listeners to bind up their shame and feel better about themselves.

Some churches have developed the habit of focusing on themselves. Not always, but many times, this is because as a group they have been infected with shame and so have become self-centered. The members are comfortable with each other. They know one another, spend time together, help one another. They don't feel comfortable doing the same with people outside the church.

But Jesus associated with sinners. His enemies criticized him as a glutton and a drunkard. Obviously he didn't go to such excess, but the accusation would not even have occurred to his enemies if Jesus had only met with his followers. Jesus called us the salt of the earth. What if the salt never gets out of the saltshaker? Our self-centeredness could have eternal negative implications in the lives of our neighbors who very much need someone to love them. Does the level of shame in your life leave you free to love sinners, even if religious people gossip about you and smear your name because of it?

Barriers for unbelievers

If shame can bottle up Christians like this, the effect for unbelievers is even stronger. There are two mortal traps that shame throws in the way to keep unbelievers from coming to Christ. If we can recognize these barriers against faith, we may be able to find a way to love the people into the Kingdom.

The first trap is set for those who have chosen the hard way of defending themselves against shame. They have the problem that they can't admit to any weakness, or even that they might have been wrong about something. They need to be self-sufficient and always in the right. If they have a lot of ability and education, the situation might be even more difficult, because they are used to knowing more than everyone else.

The problem is that Christianity is exclusively for those who have been wrong. He who conceals his sins does not prosper, but whoever confesses and renounces them finds mercy (Proverbs 28:13). In order to come to Christ, you have to confess that you are going wrong and need His help to get out of your mess. This is a very high barrier to anyone who feels he has to be right. We can't change the requirements for salvation, but we can change our way of presenting the Gospel.

Jesus healed a man who had been born blind (the story is in John 9:1-41). The religious leaders of the day couldn't heal anybody, so Jesus' action made them look inadequate in comparison. He was also showing them up with his teaching and his popularity with the people.

The situation after the healing was tense but manageable up until the healed man asked the religious leaders if they also wanted to be disciples of Jesus. This hit them directly in the shame spot, because they were already desperately defending their position as guardians of the access to God. They responded to this attack on their dignity with insults, trying to shame the man. He tried to reason logically with them. But trying to reason with people who know they are wrong and are becoming emotional about it shames them even more. The logical argument of an obviously uneducated person makes them look ignorant, because of course he is right. The result is fury.

Up until this point, they could have repented and fixed things up with Jesus, but instead they threw the healed man out of the synagogue with more insults. Jesus said that their guilt remained, because they insisted that they knew and were right. Needing to be right can be deadly.

As you might have guessed, I had adopted for the most part the hard defense against shame. The friends who loved me to Christ handled the situation well. I surely would have fled the group if they had insisted that I admit to being a sinner. I was very much into having to be right, and I also considered myself to be much more righteous than most of the other students at that public university. But my friends didn't push me on this. They just kept loving me and teaching me to study the Bible, so I stayed, and eventually the Holy Spirit could do the convincing they could not have done. If another human being had told me I was wrong I would have reacted strongly. It was more difficult to refuse the conviction of God, who knew me perfectly. Not pushing a self-righteous person to admit sin may seem like being soft on him, and it certainly may take longer than one might like for the process to be complete, but in reality it is only the conviction of the Holy Spirit that counts.

The other trap is for those who choose the soft defense against shame. The danger here is more subtle. Many of these people protect themselves by serving. They have possibly been earning brownie points like this for most of their life, and often can't imagine a relationship that is not based on other people's being grateful for their work. When they become convinced of the truth of Christ's death and resurrection and that He wants to live in their lives, they receive Him with enthusiasm and immediately go to work for Him. Normally a church needs people who will work, so nobody questions the motives for their service. But many times they are trying to win their salvation in the same way that they earn their acceptance by other people.

In a church I knew well, someone invited a neighbor, an elderly lady, to attend services. Much to everyone's surprise, the woman quickly made a profession of faith, and immediately started giving and working. She was careful to tithe; she gave the pastor, a talented musician, a new guitar; she volunteered to clean the church; she fixed delicious food for church suppers. But she still seemed to be troubled. Finally it came out that she still wondered if she was doing enough, if God would accept the offerings she was making as sufficient. She knew that she didn't have much more time to live, and wanted to make sure she was going to heaven. When she finally understood that her salvation didn't depend on her giving and working, she was incredulous at first, but then overjoyed. She did stop working quite so hard, but her joy bubbled over onto everyone and accomplished much more than her slavish work had.

It can be difficult to convince people like this that their salvation depends on Christ alone. If they are heavily infected with shame, they may have a lot of trouble with self-condemnation. Just as they would clean their house before inviting someone to have coffee, they want to clean up their lives first before having Jesus come in. So they work, and they try self-improvement. The result is that there are many people in the churches who can talk good theology, who tell anyone how much they love the Lord, who work hard and serve others with much dedication, but who are spiritually dead inside. They don't really believe that God loves them as they are, and they have never had a real encounter with Jesus.

But be careful here. The service that they give probably does help others, even if it is also to help themselves, so it isn't all bad. The goal is not to eliminate service, nor to go around questioning the motives of everyone who serves, but to identify the shame and root it out. Serving others is good. Jesus said to serve others. We shouldn't use service (in and of itself) as a way of deciding if we or anyone else is using it as a way to hide shame.

Although I have mentioned the need to be always right and the need to earn worthiness as barriers to conversion, shame-prone people do show up in churches and may attend for many years without anyone personally talking to them about either of these problems. Being active in a church does not fix the problem. I know people who at one time or another must have confessed sin in order to convince others of their conversion, but who haven't admitted to being wrong about anything else since then. They do a great job of propagating shame in the Church. Some of them are pastors.

I also have sat with the pastor of a growing, successful church who had to take a year off from his pastorate because he was completely burned out and depressed. He felt compelled to work every waking minute, since he thought that God would not be pleased with him otherwise. When I started to talk to him about how God had saved him out of love, not in order to get work out of him, he shook his head. When I told him about God's love and salvation by grace and not by works, he smiled weakly and recognized that I was preaching the Gospel to him, as he had preached it to so many others. But although he gave intellectual consent to this, he was still bound by shame. The story has a happy ending, in that he was able to overcome his shame in the way we will describe in Chapter 6, and now he is in a position to help in the liberation of others.

Pride

Pride and shame are usually considered to be complete opposites. But it turns out that they can be two sides of the same coin.

For the moment let us consider pride as the over-inflated opinion some people have of themselves, believing that they are much better than they really are. We will be modifying this definition shortly. This kind of pride is very different from "good pride," such as the satisfaction we feel when we have done a good job, or a general feeling of self-acceptance and worthiness. Too many Christians have been taught to think of themselves as proud when they feel good about themselves for having done well. Accusing someone of pride for rejoicing in who God made him to be is actually shaming him.

Shame and pride tend to come together in the actions of shame-prone people as they try to defend themselves against the pain of shame. A person who uses the strong method of hiding shame may criticize others or try to control them. Those who receive this treatment normally consider that such a person is proud. This is especially true if he cannot accept correction or if he constantly imposes himself as an authority over others. It looks like pride to others who are his victims, but he actually feels inferior.

On the other hand, those who use the supposedly weak defense impose not their authority but their help on others, whether the others have asked for it or not. Often this produces the agreeable sensation for the "helper" of being superior. The "helped" often feel it as a put-down, which it is. They are being viewed as incompetent and needing help. This provokes them to judge the helper as "proud".

It seems unjust and irrational, or even cruel, to accuse someone of being proud if the dialogue going around in his head accuses him of being inferior, a dialogue which comes out of fear and a lack of confidence in himself. The most notable characteristic of pride, though, is a self-promoting self-centeredness. Since this is also a main characteristic of those who are defending themselves against shame, it is very difficult for you to know whether you are being put down and controlled by a proud person or a shamed person. It looks and feels exactly the same from the outside.

The humility necessary to consider others better than ourselves, let others have power over our life, and accept correction, is very valuable. It permits us to live in community. But attaining such humility is hard for shame-prone people. Their every instinct is to protect themselves in a way that others may see as proud.

God says that He opposes the proud, but gives grace to the humble (James 4:6, Proverbs 3:34). If we permit ourselves the luxury of defending our sense of shame in a proud way, God himself will resist us. He commands us to humble ourselves under His mighty hand, so that He may exalt us in due time (I Peter 5:6). As Rick Joyner has explained in his book, *Epic Battles of the Last Days*, "it is our job to humble ourselves and it is the Lord's job to do the exalting. It is clear that if we try to do His job He will do our job, and He can do either one of them much better than we can."

God is not against shamed people. He is against those who exalt themselves. Exalting oneself could come from shame, or it could come from an excessively high self evaluation. When this conduct affects the life of other people, it feels the same to them whether it is pride or shame. If you are rude to me, it hurts me just the same whether you feel poorly about yourself or overly impressed with yourself. Proud conduct puts others down, shaming them and thus propagating shame in the community.

Those who defend themselves with the soft method might fall into another pride trap. There is a healthy pride, the sort of "self love" that gives one a correct view of one's identity and abilities, accompanied by a certain satisfaction in those good aspects of who one is. Some churches teach that we ought not to consider ourselves good in any way. They cite Paul, who wrote in Romans 7:18, "I know that nothing good lives in me, that is, in my sinful nature", and teach that anything that could seem good in us is fatally contaminated with sin. According to this way of thinking, if I think I am good or that I have done something good, I commit the sin of pride. Those who defend themselves by the weak tactic agree, and so does the general culture of women.

But Paul was not saying in this passage that there was nothing at all good in him, because he said that his desires were good! (verse 22). Also in verse 25 he says that in his mind he is a slave to God's law. This is good! Then in I Corinthians 11:1 he exhorts believers to be imitators of him, as he is an imitator of Christ. Telling someone to imitate what you are and do is proclaiming that there is something good in you which merits being imitated! Paul has not declared himself bad, useless, and worthless. Although he has a natural tendency to sin, the work of Christ in him has produced something valuable. The question then is not whether one is permitted to say that something is good about oneself. The question is whether it is true that there is something good, and in what way we acknowledge that.

We need to know the truth about ourselves. The Lord tells us to think about ourselves with sober judgment, in accordance with the measure of faith God has given us (Romans 12:3). That means we need to have an accurate concept of who we are, what we can do, and what God wants to do through us. The context of this commandment is that we should not think more highly of ourselves than is justified. That is pride. But to believe that we are less than what we really are is also a lack of good judgment. It may be to deny the good that the Lord himself has done in us. Straying from the truth in either direction is a bad estimate of who we are, because it can motivate us to defend ourselves or promote ourselves in an improper way.

This teaching that we need to deny the good in ourselves has had some very bad effects on the Church. The first effect is not very visible, but it is profound. When we preach that believers are totally bad, we propagate toxic shame in the Church. The Church should be a place to receive healing and deliverance, but in some cases it has become a source of shame.

The other bad effect of this teaching is to convince people who could serve the Lord with their gifts not to believe that they have any worthwhile gifts, so they don't do anything. The extended context of the passage in Romans 12 has to do with using the gifts God has given each one of us in order to serve. If I can't admit that I have any gifts or that I do anything well, how can I presume to use any gifts? If I don't have anything good to offer, I can't do anything. The result of this is that, even though the Scripture says that the Spirit has distributed at least one gift to every believer (I Corinthians 12:11), the body of Christ often ends up lame, deaf, mute, and lifeless.

Carolyn E. Kerr

I can never forgive myself

Many shame-prone people have very high expectations for themselves, which is not surprising if they think they have to be perfect to be acceptable. If then they do not live up to their own norms the results may be traumatic for them.

Suppose that a highly shame-prone person commits a grave error, and everyone knows it. For example, a devoted mother doesn't see her two-year-old behind the car as she backs up, and runs over her own child. An elder in the church commits adultery. A young single woman who is against abortion finds herself pregnant and without support for motherhood and elects to abort her baby. A leader in the youth group starts to run around with a gang of fast friends and ends up dealing drugs. A pastor sees that a man in the congregation seems depressed and probably needs a pastoral visit, but he doesn't really like the man and keeps putting off the visit, until finally the man commits suicide.

Horrified by the consequences of what he has done, the person confesses his error or sin, laments it at length, shows great anxiety, and says that he can never forgive himself. It would be difficult to doubt the sincerity of this confession, made with tears and anguish, especially when the anguish continues for months or even years.

The Christian counsel that such people generally receive is that they need to accept the forgiveness that God offers them in the sacrifice of Christ on the cross. The blood of Christ cleanses us from all sin when we confess it. This is the theologically correct answer. Nevertheless the counsel often doesn't solve the problem for the shame-prone person, even though the person agrees that it is correct. Why can't he forgive himself if God has forgiven him? Are his norms for himself higher than God's norms?

In a certain sense, that may be the problem. He cannot deny having done something wrong. But if he refuses to forgive himself, he can assert that he is really not the kind of person who would do such a thing. By accident, in the weakness of a moment, he has failed, but let nobody think he is a bad person because of it. Especially he doesn't want to believe that himself. He admits no character deficiency.

So he has repented only of his momentary failing. He has not admitted for a moment that he is like everyone else, a sinner. If he forgave himself, he would have to lower his own standards and admit to being imperfect. But he wants to continue with the illusion of perfection. So what looks so very humble is really a manifestation of pride. He requires more than God does in order to forgive. It is a way of confessing guilt—when there is no way to deny it—without confessing to being the kind of person who would do whatever he did.

In 2 Corinthians 7:8-10 Paul explains that when we respond to a rebuke, when we have to take responsibility for our sin, we can sense one of two kinds of sadness. In a previous letter, Paul had rebuked the Corinthians for having permitted certain sins within the church, and now he comments on the way they reacted to his rebuke: "Even if I caused you sorrow by my letter, I do not regret it. Though I did regret it—I see that my letter hurt you, but only for a little while—yet now I am happy, not because you were made sorry, but because your sorrow led you to repentance. For you became sorrowful as God intended and so were not harmed in any way by us. Godly sorrow brings repentance that leads to salvation and leaves no regret, but worldly sorrow brings death." There is godly sorrow and worldly sorrow.

The right kind of sorrow, according to God's plan, leads us to repentance and freedom from guilt. But there is another kind of sorrow, which is also genuine sorrow, which is motivated not by guilt but by shame. That kind of sorrow lets us come out with our dignity intact, with the face we put out to the public free of mud, and with our own opinion of ourselves undamaged. We have only to continue lamenting what we have done in order to prove that we really are good people.

This kind of sadness does protect against some of the pain of shame, but it can lead to depression. If the person doesn't realize what she is doing and repent, not only of the original act but also of her protective pseudo-confession afterward, she could be tied up for life. She may never have the blessing of sensing that God has really forgiven her. In covering up her shame, she may condemn herself to continue suffering.

Another reason that people may not be able to forgive themselves is that they insist on fixing their own guilt. They are responsible people. They pay their taxes and their debts and do their duty wherever they see it. If they hurt someone they will try to make amends. They don't want to see themselves as recipients of charity, even if it is God's charity. If they have sinned, they need to suffer, and if they have sinned greatly there may be no way they can suffer enough. The Roman Catholic ritual of penance may help these people feel like they have paid. If not, there are also sects where they can flagellate themselves to pay by their suffering. Whether they flagellate themselves physically or not, they can make themselves very miserable if their pride will not allow them to take a benefit they have not paid for.

In C. S. Lewis's classic, *The Great Divorce*, a busload of people from Hell visit Heaven. People the visitors knew on earth and who are now in Heaven try to convince them to stay instead of going back to Hell. That turns out to be harder than one would think. One of the visitors is a man who rejects the offer to stay by affirming that he won't accept anybody's bleeding charity. Unfortunately that is the only way we will get into heaven, by accepting the Bleeding Charity that the Lord offers.

Envy

Envy is the direct opposite of gratitude. It is the only one of the seven mortal sins that tries to destroy something good simplybecause it is good. We know that Cain murdered Abel precisely because Abel's works were good (I John 3:11-12).

Shame-prone people find it much easier to cry with someone who has suffered some loss or defeat than to rejoice with someone who has been victorious. They can feel superior to people who suffer, so they can relate to them better. They might even be able to help them! But it is much more difficult to celebrate someone else's victory, success, or anything that has gone well, especially if it is something that they would have wanted also for themselves. Or maybe not "also" but rather "instead of" the other person.

We are not all alike, and sometimes the other guy gets ahead of us. Shame-prone people want to be the best, to control the situation, and they may feel threatened by someone with better luck, greater success, more and better stuff, or more power. There are two ways to remove this inequality: improve their own position or, if they can't do that, destroy the other person.

Why would I feel envy toward another person? Wouldn't it be because I was discontent with what I am or have? If I were really content with myself and my life, I wouldn't have problems with the good fortune of others. But if believe I lack something, envy is waiting to pounce on me, because shame tells me that I am inferior not only because I don't have whatever it is, but also because I don't deserve to have it. Instead of working to correct whatever is lacking in our own lives, we start saying the desired thing is worthless (sour grapes attitude) or attacking the person who has it.

Jesus was the motive of envy for many people.

The chief priests and the Pharisees interpreted the miracles that Jesus did as a threat (John 11:45-48). They tried to kill Lazarus after his resurrection because the miracle was causing many people to believe in Jesus. They were afraid that if Jesus continued doing such wonderful things, everybody would believe in him.

They said that then the Romans would come and take away their place (Greek: *topos*) and their nation. The most important thing was probably the possibility that if the people believed in Jesus, they could lose their preeminence, even without the intervention of the Romans. The Greek word "*topos*", sometimes interpreted as referring to the temple, can also mean "social position" and "office". They could lose their authority over the people, and that was a scary thought to them.

Jesus made them look incompetent and powerless. They felt they had to eliminate him before his identity as the Messiah could destroy the comfortable life they had achieved. Envy of Jesus' popularity thus became the motive to kill him. Pilate knew that it was out of envy that they had handed Jesus over to him (Matthew 27:18).

The religious leaders succeeded in killing Jesus, but that did not end their problems with envy. In Acts 5:17-41 we learn that the chief priest and other Sadducees were filled with jealousy because of the miracles that the apostles did and the growing multitude of people who followed them. Nobody was trying to follow the priests. So they arrested the apostles and put them in jail. The Lord brought the apostles out of jail miraculously, thus shaming the leaders even more. When Peter preached a short version of his Pentecost sermon, they were not moved to repentance, but rather became furious. Gamaliel managed to calm them showing them that they would have less shame if they just let Jesus' followers go in peace. The apostles rejoiced that they were worthy to suffer because of Christ.

But this was not the end of the shame and envy of the Jewish leaders. In Acts 7:51-8:1 we read that Stephen, at the end of his defense in front of the Sanhedrin, shamed his accusers. He accused them of following in the footsteps of those who had killed the prophets. Reacting with fury, they lost all control of themselves, dragged him out of the city and began to stone him. Men of such high station should not have had to react so strongly to the ranting of an uneducated and insignificant preacher. It would be more logical for them to just shuffle him off to jail and forget about him. The problem was that he was telling the truth, and they knew it, and they were shamed. The over-reaction of starting a persecution of the believers in Jesus is evidence that the men of the Sanhedrin knew that they were wrong. Calling shame-prone people to account like that can seriously damage your health.

In Acts 13:44-50, the apostle Paul is preaching in Antioch of Pisidia, where, "almost the whole city gathered to hear the word of the Lord. When the Jews saw the crowds, they were filled with jealousy and talked abusively against what Paul was saying" (13:44-45). Paul and Barnabas answered them, interpreting their reaction as the result of rejection of the word of God, and told them, "you . . . do not consider yourselves worthy of eternal life" (verse 46). Not considering oneself to be worthy is practically a definition of shame. The Jews felt envy because Paul was attracting more of the public than they were. In this case shame has resulted not only in the persecution of those who were preaching, but also in the exclusion from eternal life of those who were prisoners of shame. In order to treat envy, you have to treat shame.

It is possible in a society where there are many shame-prone people that a vicious circle can get going where envious reactions of some people produce more and more shame, which produces more and more envy. In Ecclesiastes 4:4 we read, "I saw that all labor and all achievement spring from man's envy of his neighbor. This too is meaningless, a chasing after the wind." Other translations turn this around a bit saying "all work and all achievement awakens the envy of a man against his neighbor." The original has no verb, and because of this both translations are equally valid, though one says that work provokes envy and the other says that envy provokes work. Work and excellence can both produce envy as well as be the result of it. If I envy someone, I may work hard to outdo him. If I manage to do that, other people may envy me. Even the same person might envy me back. While this could theoretically produce a lot of good work, the most usual result is bitter rivalry. In this way envy can self-propagate.

Circulating on the Internet is a short description of how to make enemies. All you have to do is be intelligent, elegant, sincere, light-hearted, honest, and happy. Help everyone. Love everyone. Prosper. Then you will see.

But suppose I envy someone and there is no way I can outdo them. Suppose I feel shamed by their success because I don't have the same success, and there is nothing I can do about it. I may become angry. Angry people often do irrational things.

I remember one day when I was little that my father came home from work very upset. For the first time in his life he had won something in a raffle, and he brought with him the fancy high-powered lantern which was his prize. But he wasn't happy. Some of the other men at work had envied his luck and had poured their coffee with cream into it to ruin it. He was never able to make the lantern work after that.

In James 3:14-16 we see that "if you harbor bitter envy and selfish ambition in your hearts, do not boast about it or deny the truth. Such 'wisdom' does not come down from heaven but is earthly, unspiritual, of the devil. For where you have envy and selfish ambition, there you find disorder and every evil practice."

Hypocrisy in the Church

A church infected with shame cannot live in peace with itself, and much less reach others with a message of love and acceptance. Besides, the social customs of the church sometimes contribute to the infection of shame by encouraging everyone to be "fine".

Even though everyone in the church might have excellent theology and all admit they are sinners and do not reach the perfection of the glory of Christ, they don't want anybody to find out if they really fall into sin. It is important not to lose face, to keep on with the "triumphant Christian" pose. Especially those who announce that the Lord can heal the wounds of the soul and help us triumph over our circumstances don't want anyone to know when they have been humiliated, because they would be shamed by admitting defeat.

So when we go to church we put on our all-is-well masks. Everyone is fine—just ask them. If I admit I am not fine I may soon find myself criticized, looked down on, isolated, pitied, or removed from the view of those who maintain an artificial positive attitude. Some may reproach me for my lack of faith, or treat me as a spiritual incompetent, but they may not give me the support I need. If help is offered it will be with a condescending attitude by someone who would never admit to having problems. Each person does have his or her own internal pain, but if I judge by the happy faces of everyone else, I may come to the conclusion that I am the only one that feels bad. This shames me even more.

This hypocrisy produces churches full of people in pain who proclaim that there is an answer, but in reality they never receive it. The Gospel supposedly heals, but the reality is that many times people do not receive the healing they need in the church. The natural result of this is double-think. My theology says one thing but my experience says another. I go on proclaiming the theology, but my enthusiasm has to cool down when I come to the conclusion that it doesn't work for me. It must be that my faith is deficient, I am ashamed to admit. I may even get to the point where I am spiritually numb and can no longer respond to the presence of God.

One result of this double-think is that we lose our spiritual power. In James 1:6-8 we read that such doubt puts us in a position where we cannot pray with faith and we mustn't expect to receive anything. Another result is that we will not be so quick to share how our marvelous Lord has transformed our life.

The results of this hypocrisy don't stay within the church, either. Outsiders can see it very clearly, especially if they are looking for excuses to reject the message. The Swiss physician, Paul Tournier, in his book,

The Healing of Persons, has described this very well. "A lot of religious people pretend to be free of sins and passions from which they have not been freed. This is to hide their lack of a genuine experience with Jesus. Unbelievers can see this, and they don't want to be like them."

The world, the flesh . . . and the devil?

If the spiritual consequences of being habitually under the influence of shame are so great, we can be sure that the devil, our spiritual enemy, is interested in taking advantage of shame to conquer the church. Some Christians today no longer believe in the devil, but Jesus knew he existed and got people freed from his emissaries. The apostles' experiences in the book of Acts show that they fought against a very real, though invisible enemy, and triumphed. Our modern scientific mindset has led many Christians to reject this teaching, but we need to take the devil seriously, neither ignoring him nor being afraid, nor attributing more power to him than he really has. His biggest weapon against us is deception, getting us to believe and act on lies.

Shame provides him with whole packs of lies to get us tied up in knots. He can entice us to believe those hurtful lies we bring with us from childhood, convince us that sin won't hurt us or anyone else, get us focusing on ourselves instead of on Jesus or on helping our neighbors, or any number of other tempting thoughts. In reality, using shame on us the enemy can get a triple reward for the sin to which he himself incites us, or from the pain that others cause us.

First, shame can get in the way of our taking our guilt and pain to the Lord in order to receive forgiveness and healing. If we don't even want to confess our guilt to the Lord, how much less will we confess it to our brothers and sisters so they can help us overcome sin! So shame separates us from the freedom we could have in Christ.

The *second* benefit that the enemy has from our shame is to accuse us of our condition, so as to discourage us and push us toward depression. Shame, merited or not, produces an attitude that underscores our weaknesses and lack of worth. It converts a specific sin into a condemnation of our whole being. Even though we are created in the image of God, crowned with glory and honor, part of the spotless Bride of Christ, holy and beloved, when our thoughts constantly accuse us, it is hard to accept the identity that Christ has given us. This is a situation that the Accuser of the brethren thinks is delightful.

One technique that the enemy uses to sink us in our shame is to pretend to be the voice of the Holy Spirit. The Holy Spirit convicts us of sin (John 16:8), but the enemy accuses us (Revelation 12:10). The enemy accuses us before God, but he also accuses us to ourselves. He reminds us of how bad we are, and sees to it that we hear it often. Our conscience is malleable and not always reliable. If we aren't careful, the two voices, that of the Holy Spirit and that of the enemy, can sound a bit similar, since they are both pointing out something wrong with us.

The key to knowing the difference is that the Holy Spirit speaks in specific terms. He shows us our guilt for some specific action. He says, "You shouldn't have done that. Stop it. Repent. Repair the damage you have done. Don't do it again." This produces sadness, but in a healthy way, and it permits us to start again. But the enemy accuses us in general terms, such as "You are bad. You always mess up. You will never be able to overcome this habit." The Holy Spirit doesn't condemn us globally nor suggest that we will never get out of our hole.

The *third* benefit that the enemy gets from our shame is that in our painful condition he uses us to hurt others and get them to suffer the same way. In the pain of our shame, we shame others. So he can destroy not only our fellowship with the Lord but with other believers, too. He can prevent us from walking in the power and authority which should be ours and effectively prevent any possibility that we might win others to Christ.

The danger of evil spirits is real. Our enemy is alive and among us. In a controversial but discerning vision which Rick Joyner has published in his book, The Final Quest, he saw armies of demons marching against the Church in the end times. They went to battle under the flags of "Pride," "Self Righteousness," "Respectability," "Selfish Ambition," "Unfair Judgment," and "Envy." It is notable that the banners are specifically symptoms of shame. The weapons that this army of demons carried were primarily those which use the tongue. As the Lord warns us in James 3:6, "The tongue also is a fire, a world of evil among the parts of the body. It corrupts the whole person, sets the whole course of his life on fire, and is itself set on fire by hell." This army is marching against the Church today. We should not be surprised, then, when we find accusations, gossip, libel, and complaints in the Church, along with intimidation and betrayal. We should not be surprised, and we should resist.

The army that Joyner saw in his vision was marching specifically against the Church. The demons were riding on the backs of Christians, with the purpose of causing divisions at all levels of the Church. Reconnaissance troops went first to find weak points that they could take advantage of in churches, families or individuals. These explorers had a lot of power and had authority to "baptize en masse" with Rejection, Bitterness, Impatience, Lack of forgiveness, or Lust. Just one demon could spread his poison over a whole race or culture. In the vision of Joyner, Christians who served as horses for the demons were convinced that they were doing the work of the Lord with their slander, complaining, and intimidation. They themselves carried banners of Self-Righteousness.

When some evil things are present in a community, they can propagate themselves. Bitterness produces more bitterness (Hebrews 12:15). Rejection produces more rejection. Lack of forgiveness generates more lack of forgiveness. Shame produces more shame. Once the process gets started, the natural tendency is for it to get worse, given our fallen human tendency to repay others with the same treatment we have received or worse. If there is also diabolic energy behind the process, the results can be a disaster.

That there might be a deliberate diabolic attack against the day-to-day life of the Church is a chilling thought. Some people would rather just decide that the devil doesn't exist. But the evidence is there. "Be self-controlled and alert. Your enemy the devil prowls around like a roaring lion looking for someone to devour. Resist him, standing firm in the faith . . ." (I Peter 5:8-9. We need to wake up to the danger and learn to defend ourselves.

Unity among believers

Jesus has entered into his glory. But he said in his last prayer for his disciples in John 17:22, "I have given them the glory that you gave me, that they may be one as we are one." Considered just from a logical point of view, this phrase is difficult to understand. What does glory have to do with the disciples being as one or not? But from the point of view of shame, it is easily understood. A real union between persons must come from mutual understanding and acceptance. This is only possible if the persons are free of shame so that they can rightfully consider other people. When people are conscious of having received the glory of Christ, they are more able to understand and accept others, assuming that they recognize that what they have received they have received by grace, not through their own merits. When we know who we really are we can relate to one another without the complications of envy and rivalry. We can be one.

Questions for reflection:

1. Did shame play any role in your conversion experience? If shame was a barrier to your coming to Christ, how did you overcome it? Is there something that other believers could have done to help you?
2. How can we acquire a balanced estimation of who we are and what we can do?
3. Do you have high standards for the way you live? If so, how do you react to people who do not have such high standards? How do you get along with people who do have high standards? Has there been a time when you could not live up to your own norms? What was the result of that?
4. Think of a time when you felt envy. What lack in your own life could have inspired you to envy someone else? What were the results of envy for you personally? What were the results of your envy in other people?

5. Has anyone ever attacked you and you suspected that they were envious of you? How did you respond to the attack? What were the results for you and for others?

6. Is everyone fine in your church? Or do they say they are? How can people who need spiritual help get it without having to feel criticized or looked down on?

CHAPTER 5 **Jesus, Man without Shame**

If anyone ever had reason to feel shame, it was Jesus.

He came from a poor family in a small country occupied by foreign forces. Even the region where he was brought up was despised by people in the rest of the country. Upon first hearing of Jesus, a man who would later become one of his disciples reacted by saying, "Can anything good come out of Nazareth?"

His mother had conceived him out of wedlock, a fact well known to any neighbor able to count to nine, and even the man who later would be considered to be his father at first doubted the fantastic tale his mother told about an angel. His younger brothers did not believe that Jesus was anyone special. His fellow townspeople tried to kill him.

Although he was a carpenter, he lived as an itinerant preacher, eating and sleeping however and wherever he could. The poor people followed him, but the important men of his day and the leaders of the spiritual establishment soundly rejected him. He was known for associating with prostitutes, revolutionaries, corrupt government officials and other unsavory characters. He was publicly mocked as a glutton and drunkard.

He was said to be shameless.

But he wasn't. He was shame-free, which is exactly the opposite.

Jesus had come to his own place, since as the second person of the Trinity he had participated in Creation. One would expect that the Chosen People of God would receive him with enthusiasm. But they rejected him, even though he had come to help them. It is probable that he knew when he came that they would not respond well, since the prophecies of the Old Testament plainly describe the Servant of the Lord who suffers rejection. "He was despised and rejected by men, a man of sorrows, and familiar with suffering" (Isaiah 53:3).

God had previously modeled humility for his people for centuries. We read in Isaiah 65:1-3 that the Lord had put up with the insults and provocations of his people, but continued to be willing for the people to find him even when they didn't look for him. He continued to call to them, holding out his hands to a rebellious people. Jesus did the same when he came to the earth. Even someone who despises him is allowed to repent if he wants to. We have to conclude that it is a characteristic of God not to respond harshly to rejection. Offering love and acceptance to those who despise you does not prove that their opinion of you is correct. On the contrary, it is being God-like.

Jesus came with the right to rule in the world, but of his own accord he laid aside that right. "Who, being in very nature God, did not consider equality with God something to be grasped, but made himself nothing, taking the very nature of a servant, being made in human likeness" (Philippians 2:6-7). The shock of finding himself subject to the human condition must have been very strong, but his manner of handling that it was very different from the reaction of those who feel shame at being humiliated. When they tried to throw him off a cliff, instead of responding with fury he just walked away. When they accused him of casting out demons by the prince of demons, he responded with logical arguments. Although he made who he was very clear and denounced sin wherever he found it, he did so with serene, controlled and reasonable authority. His opponents, on the other hand, frequently became furious. They were afraid.

John the Baptist had no difficulty in accepting Jesus' ministry as better than his own because he knew his own identity and that of Jesus. He rejoiced to hear the voice of the Bridegroom. This contrasts with the attitude of the Important Men of the time, who saw the miracles and how the people came to Jesus, but reacted with envy. They knew perfectly well who Jesus was, but did not want to accept humbly their rightful position under his authority.

Nicodemus and Joseph of Arimathea, and possibly Gamaliel, were exceptions. The Jews began to plot his death because he supposedly violated the Sabbath and because he called God his father, making himself equal to God (John 5:17-18). If he had said this without having done miracles, perhaps they would just have looked down on him as a harmless crazy man. But the truth about his identity hit them right in the shame, since they couldn't do the same miracles, and especially since the people didn't flock after them.

Jesus did not depend on public opinion to know who he was. In John 5:41-44 he said that he didn't accept praise from men, as his adversaries did. His identity was not based on what other people said about him. Those who criticized him attached much importance to their mutual affirmation and praise. But Jesus' authority came from his relationship with his Father, something that they did not have.

Dependency on human acceptance makes you susceptible to the effects of shame, because at any moment the acceptance may cease. This is especially important for you if you are having success in what you do, because the envy of others will reduce the public affirmation and may provoke slander and persecution.

The reason why Jesus could humble himself so much is made evident in John 13:3-5. The context is the Last Supper with his disciples. Jesus got up, took off his outer clothing, tied on a towel, and started to wash the feet of the disciples. He was doing the job of a low-ranking slave. He was not defending his rank as the leader of the group. The disciples clearly felt that this action was inappropriate for him, but he insisted.

In the third verse we can begin to discover the reason he could do this. "Jesus knew that the Father had put all things under his power, and that he had come from God and was returning to God; so he got up . . . ." Jesus knew who he was. He knew that he had all power, all authority. He knew that he had come from God and was returning to God. He didn't have to prove anything to anybody, and even less did he have to prove anything to himself. His identity did not depend on being in a position of authority nor acting like an important person, nor on what anyone else would say or think. His capacity for humility was based on being sure of who he was, and sure of his relationship with God, and on knowing the great purpose that had brought him to earth.

This knowledge was the perfect defense against shame. It was important that he have such a defense, because a few hours after the Supper, his enemies would do as much as they could to shame him. Today, when we meditate on what Jesus suffered for us, we usually concentrate on the physical suffering, on how he died in a very painful way as a sacrifice for our sins. Without lessening the importance of this truth, we can also appreciate what he must have suffered emotionally.

The writer of the letter to the Hebrews understood very well the importance of this when he wrote: "Jesus, the author and perfecter of our faith, . . . for the joy set before him endured the cross, scorning its shame, and sat down at the right hand of the throne of God. Consider him who endured such opposition from sinful men, so that you will not grow weary and lose heart" (Hebrews 12:2-3).

He was sure of his identity and had determined his purpose. He could bear not only the physical pain, but also the shaming to which they subjected him. Just looking at the account of the crucifixion in Luke, chapters 22 and 23, we can see how they tried to shame him:

He was betrayed with the kiss of one of his followers. After dedicating three years of his precious life to these men, Judas paid him out like that.

They arrested him as a common criminal. It was not a respectful process.

Peter three times denies knowing him. Even his closest followers were ashamed of him.

The soldiers made fun of him. They covered his eyes and demanded that he prophesy saying who had hit him. They were making fun of his spiritual power and authority. That was a complete rejection of his true identity.

They presented him before Pilate with false charges as someone who perverted the people. Perverted?

Herod and his soldiers insulted and mocked him, dressing him with splendid robes.

The mob preferred to free a murderer instead of him.

They led him through the streets of Jerusalem so that everyone could have a chance to mock him. This was the equivalent of scenes in a present-day newscast where they bring out a prisoner in handcuffs, but they didn't hide his face. He also had to carry his cross. People have a tendency to make fun of someone who is losing a battle.

Crucifixion is a shameful death in itself, because it is reserved for criminals. Two criminals died with Jesus, one on each side of him, giving the impression that he was the same as they were.

The soldiers divided his clothes among them. This means that they crucified him naked. In the paintings and statues that Christians have made of this scene, they always leave him a loincloth, but the Romans were not so considerate in real life. Their purpose was to shame him as much as possible. The Jews abhorred nudity for both cultural and biblical reasons. Nakedness was a component of the shame that God had promised as a punishment for those who rebelled against him. (Jeremiah 13:25-26, Deuteronomy 28:47-48).

The head men of the Jews and the soldiers, and even one of the criminals crucified with him, mocked him when he was on the cross. Once again they chose to mock his true identity, rejecting the redemptive work that he was doing in that very moment.

The people who were loyal to Jesus kept their distance. Everyone was looking at him as though he were an object, not a person.

The title that they put on the cross said that he was the King of the Jews, but it did not have the purpose of identifying him, but rather making fun of him.

Jesus commended his spirit to his Father (23:46). In doing this he finished the work he was committed to do when he first came to the earth. They humiliated him and spit on him, but they couldn't shame him. His submission was voluntary, and he received the humiliation with dignity and self-control. As the prophet Isaiah said of him, "I offered my back to those who beat me, my cheeks to those who pulled out my beard; I did not hide my face from mocking and spitting. Because the Sovereign Lord helps me, I will not be disgraced. Therefore have I set my face like a flint, and I know I will not be put to shame" (Isaiah 50:6-7).

In all of his suffering he refused to receive the shame that they threw at him. He was not ashamed. The fact that other people humiliate us does not force us to be ashamed.

It was important that Christ suffer such humiliation, because in dying on the cross he took not only your guilt, but also your shame. He identified with you in his physical death, paying the price for your sin. He also identified with you in allowing himself to be humiliated. On the cross he experienced all of the shame that you can possibly suffer, whether your shame is deserved or not.

No other sacrifice is necessary for your sins. When you confess your sins you receive forgiveness. In the same way, it is not necessary that you continue to suffer from shame. He has taken your shame on himself. As the Scripture says, "Anyone who trusts in him will never be put to shame" (Romans 10:11).

The suffering that Jesus accepted for us makes him unattractive to many people. Many people think poorly of a "savior" so weak that he can't save himself. He doesn't appear to be a triumphant hero, or even someone with whom we would like to be associated. But he carried humanity's sins, and you have to decide if you want to let him carry your personal sins. He also carried your shame. He identified himself with you, making himself as unattractive as you may sometimes think you are. In order for you to be made whole, you have to identify with him in his shame and let him carry yours, too.

Corrie ten Boom describes in *The Hiding Place* what she and her sister suffered in the Nazi concentration camps because they helped some Jews. Deliberate humiliation formed part of the suffering. One day when their captors obliged them to present themselves naked, they remembered that Jesus had been crucified naked also. They didn't have to feel humiliated because of what they were forced to do. Jesus had already passed through the same thing, and they could come to him and receive dignity instead of humiliation. They were going to accompany Jesus "outside the camp," receiving the same treatment that he had received (Hebrews 13:13).

"Therefore God exalted him to the highest place and gave him the name that is above every name, that at the name of Jesus every knee should bow, in heaven and on earth and under the earth, and every tongue confess that Jesus Christ is Lord, to the glory of God the Father" (Philippians 2:9-11).

Because of Jesus' submission to the will of God the Father in going through such humiliation, God has exalted him to the highest place. His name and position are above the whole world, and every knee will bow. We will submit ourselves to Christ, to him who has submitted himself already to much more than what we will have to put up with in this world. Will you do it now?

Questions for reflection

1. Read Philippians 2:3-8. God tells us that we should have in ourselves the same attitude that Jesus had when he voluntarily humbled himself. Why is it so hard for us to do this? Is there anything that personally holds you back?

2. What aspects of the humiliation of Jesus are similar to what you have suffered? What does it mean to you that Jesus has identified with you in these experiences?

3. Jesus could despise the shaming that he received because he was sure of his identity and purpose. Who was he? What was he doing when he died? Who are you? Do you have some purpose in your life? What is it? What has God called you to be and do? If you don't know the answer to this, ask Him to show you what it is.

4. Is there a difference between being humiliated justly or unjustly? Which bothers you more? In which of the two can we most identify with Jesus? Has God ever called you to humble yourself voluntarily?

5. What is your identity in Christ? Make a list of aspects of this identity (for example: child of God, member of the body of Christ, holy, redeemed, bride of Christ, friend of Christ, etc.). Do you feel that the descriptions on your list are really a part of your life? What changes would come to your life if they were?

CHAPTER 6 **Out from under the Cloud**

We live in a feel-good age. Medicine has given us the possibility of existing without pain, either physical or psychological. If anyone still suffers, there is a thriving market in illicit drugs that offer a variety of possibilities. They can turn you on or off, as you wish.

It is also the age of feeling good about who you are. Self-help books and videos have multiplied, giving you lots of advice about how to lift your self-esteem and free yourself of doubts and fears. They tell us we are good people and we need to believe it in order to enjoy life.

To a certain extent it works, because there are people who say they feel like they have obtained self-realization, whatever that means. But in another sense it doesn't work. Many who have learned to affirm themselves have gone too far and have become aggressive. Others have decided that the best way to realize themselves is to do whatever they want, whatever makes them feel good. Even in the church the levels of fraud, adultery, divorce, child abuse, domestic violence and drug abuse have gone up.

There are voices in the church, however, which are shouting, "Stop! What has happened to the doctrine that we are sinners and need redemption? Humanity is rebelling full tilt against God, and are we going to preach that we ought to feel good about ourselves? What we need is for the Holy Spirit to convict us of sin which will lead us to repentance and salvation!"

But it isn't so simple. Sin makes us feel bad, or at least it should, unless we have completely silenced the voice of conscience that tries to correct us. But the reverse is true, also. Shame can lead us into sin. That is what happened to Cain. We can't get rid of shame just declaring that we are good, but neither can we ignore the shame that could lead us into further difficulty.

We need a Biblical way of dealing with our problem of feeling bad about who we are.

If it is true that Jesus' death can provide us with freedom from shame, how can we acquire what he wants us to have? The number of Christians who bear up under a load of shame, anxiety and depression will not permit us to say that freedom is automatic when we turn our lives over to Christ. If it were possible to acquire spiritual and mental health in four easy steps, the problem would have been solved long ago.

If you have discovered that you have a heavy load of shame in your life, you most likely want to find a way of getting rid of the pain alone, in private, without anyone else knowing about it. But obviously if we could have done it for ourselves, Jesus would not have had to suffer as he did. Lewis Smedes, in his masterful book on shame, said about his personal struggle that everything he himself had tried in order to take away or nullify his shame had not helped at all. June Price Tangney, a psychologist who has published much research on the matter, lists various things that people could do to help themselves get rid of the shame in their lives, but later she says that she doesn't think the measures she mentions will work very well. For them to work, the person would already have to be free of shame before starting!

It seems that just like in the matter of guilt, we can't free ourselves. It has to be the grace of God that lifts us. This is true whether our shame came from our own sin, or whether it is something other people have dumped on us. This is true whether we consider shame about a specific situation or whether it is a chronic condition because we have a habit of living in shame.

If you have a lot of shame, you need to know that in spite of what you feel, or what you did, or what others did, or your opinion of yourself, or what others think, there is some important person who accepts you instead of rejecting you. The more important that person is to you, the more powerful will be the effect of this acceptance in your life. If the acceptance comes from God himself, there is an important base for the changes which need to happen, but only if you value deeply your relationship with Christ, and if this acceptance as a reality rather than just a learned doctrine.

God loves us and accepts us as his sons and daughters through Christ. Jesus accepted the sheep that were his without even the possibility of rejecting them later, saying, "My Father, who has given them to me, is greater than all; no one can snatch them out of my Fathers hand." (John 10:29). This is grace. It is a gift. There is no way we can chalk up enough points to earn it.

We have forgiveness of sin by the grace of God. Christ took on himself the punishment for our sin, and if we confess our sin He will forgive us. But apparently it is harder for us to believe that God would accept us as his children just as we are, even though our shame has been paid for along with our sin. We keep on believing that God is like everyone else, and that if we aren't perfect we aren't acceptable. We are right to believe that we don't deserve for God to notice us and accept us. It isn't a question of merit, however, but of worth. As bad as you might be, God considers that you are worth having his son die for you. Shame-prone people have a hard time believing in their worth, so they try to accumulate merit instead.

Therefore many people try to avoid dealing with their shame by putting on a good front and functioning in the church, after, of course, having admitted to past sin and "receiving Jesus as their savior". But just as with guilt, we can't get free by building up merit. If we cover up our sin, we are not freed. The same is true with shame, but it is more difficult to confess shame. If we feel guilt, this motivates us to confess, make restitution, and receive forgiveness. But shame motivates us to cover up both the fact that we have shame and the source of our shame. We don't want anyone to find out.

If we cover up our shame, we can't get rid of it.

If we cover it up in the weak manner, serving and working for Christ, perhaps wanting to qualify for God to consider us worthy of his love, we can save face in front of others in the church. But inside, we continue to have fears, anxiety, doubts, and an uncomfortable sensation that we are frauds. After a while it would really be difficult to admit our shame, especially if we have gained the respect and even the adulation of the brethren for our selfless service and humility. What on the outside appears to be humility could be a mask for not wanting to admit what we really have inside. That looks a lot like pride.

On the other hand, if we cover up our shame with the hard defense, we may convince people that we are very spiritual, capable and self-sufficient, at least for a time. But underneath there may be an anxious voice telling us that all of that could collapse in a moment if the truth got out. If anyone criticizes us, that calls into question our superiority. If someone else has more success than we do, it is possible that they might beat us in the contest of life. In either case we may respond with attacks or even fury, hurting others and sowing more shame in the community.

I John 1:5-7 shows us the importance of being transparent by walking in the light. "This is the message we have heard from him and declare to you: God is light; in him there is no darkness at all. If we claim to have fellowship with him yet walk in the darkness, we lie and do not live by the truth. But if we walk in the light, as he is in the light, we have fellowship with one another, and the blood of Jesus, his Son, purifies us from all sin." If we walk in the dark saying that we are walking in the light, we lie. If we were to walk in the light we would have communion with each other. This fellowship is exactly what we lack if we keep our secrets so as not to have to humble ourselves.

In Philippians 2:3 we read that we should consider others as better than ourselves. In the shame process, it is possible that other people have forced us to adopt this attitude. That is to say, they have obliged us to swallow the idea that we are deficient. It seems scary to a shame-prone person, but in reality the best defense against this shameful lie is to stick to the truth. If we have sinned, we should confess it. The same is true if we have failed in some way. If we really can't do something, we shouldn't deny the truth.

Jesus said that when someone accuses us and there is even a little bit of truth in the accusation, that we should come to some agreement with our accuser as soon as possible so that he doesn't take us to judgment (Matthew 5:25-27). The result of not confessing our weakness, but instead insisting on defending our innocence, is that we remain prisoners of the matter. There are people who cannot be freed of their shame because that very shame keeps them from admitting their real weakness and shame.

"Confess" means expressing our true actions, ideas and feelings. It doesn't exclusively mean admitting sin. It could mean that we open ourselves up and reveal to someone else who we really are and what we think and feel. This is what the passage in I John means about walking in the light, where everything is transparent.

So in order to get free of shame we have to do exactly the opposite of what shame makes us want to do. Instead of hiding, we have to come out in the open.

The first and most important person with whom we have to come out into the open is the Lord. He is our guide in the process, the analyst who knows our past and present, and the healer who can deal with the problem, whether we deserve our shame because of what we have done, or whether we have acquired a habit of toxic shame from others.

Deserved shame

In order to consider what to do to overcome shame, you need to figure out what kind of shame you are dealing with, whether it is a response to something you have done wrong, or whether it is shame heaped on you by others without your deserving it.

The basic solution for deserved shame is to transmute it into guilt. Guilt can be dealt with by confessing it, repenting, changing your ways, receiving forgiveness and accepting that forgiveness. God doesn't forgive your excuses. He forgives sins.

But sometimes it is hard to sort out what shame may be deserved and what not, because one of the most common means of shaming others is heaping accusations on them. If you have regularly been blamed for the negative things that happen around you, it may be difficult to sort out for which things you are guilty and for which you are not.

Especially, abused children have probably been told that it is their own fault that they have been abused. The little girl was too seductive and so was raped. The small child wouldn't stop crying so he deserved to be thrown against the wall. Children whose parents divorce usually consider themselves the cause of the breakup of the family.

In general, each person is responsible only for his or her own behavior. Parents do have responsibility for the behavior of their small children, but children are not responsible for the behavior of their parents or other adults. Neither are adults responsible for the behavior of other adults, even their spouses or adult children.

Trying to confess and repent of something you didn't do doesn't produce peace. Having to pay for something you did not steal produces a nagging feeling of injustice. Likewise trying to change in order not to be whatever you are falsely accused of being can produce constant vigilance in monitoring your behavior to make sure it "doesn't happen again", or frustrated depression, or an anxious attempt to maintain an exaggerated opposite of that characteristic.

So it is important when nagging shame tells you that you are thus-and-so to be able to discern if it really is true. For example, maybe you have been a compulsive liar, or maybe those who accuse you are the liars. Some questions you can ask yourself as you try to sort this out are:

Is there a specific behavior which triggers the shame feeling?

Is it something I have really done, or do?

Is that behavior actually wrong?

Who says that the behavior is wrong? Are they authorized to set the rules for my life? Remember that although scripture is authoritative and speaks clearly on many issues, it doesn't mention everything.

If sorting this out by yourself seems difficult, it can be very helpful to find someone else you can trust, someone who was not involved in the original dynamics, and go over the story with them. An outsider can often see clearly what is going on in our lives when the matter seems confused to us. (In the next chapter we will deal with the thorny question of how to choose someone with whom to talk about it).

If you come to the conclusion that you did do wrong and "you really ought to be ashamed of yourself," the first step out of the mud is to admit that. How you handle accusations of sin determines what your outcome will be. Jesus said that the Pharisees hated him because he pointed out their sin to them (John 7:7).

When you sin and either God himself or other people point this out, it is important to agree with the truth. Repentance, that is, a change of heart and a change of practice, will fix the matter. But yielding to the shame instead, whether covering up the sin or attacking the person who pointed out the sin, or being overwhelmed by the shame, leads to more sin. This could harden you in the position and would make future repentance more difficult. God says to Cain, "You must master sin".

Confess your sin to the Lord and ask for his forgiveness and get rid of it. If you need to make restitution for anything or apologize, do that, unless doing so would cause even more damage to the other person. (Someone once apologized to me because they had always hated me, even though I hadn't detected their hatred. I am afraid the apology didn't help our relationship much). Thank the Lord for His forgiveness and for taking your shame. In I John 1:9 we find that if we confess our sins he is faithful and just not only to forgive our sin, but also to cleanse us from all unrighteousness. Ask for that cleansing, so that the stain of guilt and shame won't be sticking around to bother you. Lift up your head and walk free.

Chronic shame

But suppose that when you ask yourself the questions above the answer to any of them is "no". Suppose that there isn't anything specific, just a general feeling that you are all wrong. Suppose that even though you are assumed to have done something, you aren't aware of having

Lift Up Your Head

done it. Suppose that you really did it, but objectively speaking it isn't wrong, just against some toxic family rules. Suppose the shame is with you all the time, affecting a large portion of your life.

In this case you are probably shame-prone and dealing with chronic, toxic shame, shame you don't deserve. Most of the shame that gives us chronic problems turns out to be something others have dumped on us. It is no good to convert this shame into guilt and try to repent of a sin you have not committed. You also cannot repent of being what you aren't supposed to be, since just wishing you were not so and determining to change probably won't produce change.

Look back at what Jesus did for us. He accepted shame he didn't deserve, carrying our shame to the cross. He did it to identify with us. He shared the fellowship of our sufferings. In Philippians 3, Paul talks about the fellowship of sharing in Christ's sufferings, but Christ shared in ours first. He allowed people to spit on him to accompany you. He did it "for the joy that was set before him" (Hebrews 12:2-3), thinking ahead to you, free, with your head held high, not growing weary and discouraged. Thank him for what he has done and ask him to accompany you in your daily walk.

Let us review what we said about how Jesus was able to defend himself against shame. He knew who he was. He knew that he had all power, all authority. He knew that he had come from God and was returning to God. He didn't have to prove anything to anybody, and even less did he have to prove anything to himself. His identity did not depend on being in a position of authority nor acting like an important person, nor on what anyone else would say or think. His capacity for humility was based on being sure of who he was, and sure of his relationship with God, and on knowing the great purpose that had brought him to earth.

Who are you? Do you have any idea? Jesus was able to complete his mission without yielding to the shame being heaped on him partly by knowing for sure who he was. In the same way, your strength in resisting shame will come from knowing who you really are in Christ.

There is a lot of mystical thinking about discovering who you "really" are, but it is not so mysterious as some make it out to be. Who you are in the ordinary sense is a combination of the kind of information that might appear at the top of some form you are filling out. Your identity may be a result of where and when you were born, and who your parents are. It may be physical characteristics such as gender, your level of intelligence, or any special abilities or disabilities you may have. It may be an acquired identity, such as your profession, your religion, your marital status, studies you have completed, your political party, and the football team you prefer.

For instance, you may be a 47-year-old Canadian man, blind but a university graduate, employed as a high school English teacher, who also pastors a small church. Or you may be a Japanese woman naturalized as a U.S. citizen, married mother of three, living in Sandusky, Ohio, and a loyal Indians fan. Or you may have been born and raised in an inner-city slum, first arrested for drug dealing at age 15, and now serving time for robbery.

As a result of who you are in that ordinary sense you may have learned certain patterns of behavior, for instance how women are "supposed to" act, what Mexican-Americans do on May 5, or how to program a computer. Privileges, responsibilities, and limitations are very often connected with our identities. If you are a citizen of a country and are of age, you may be able to vote. If you are a waitress you have to get people their coffee. If you are very near-sighted you must wear glasses in order to drive.

Who you are, or more importantly who you think you are, will also determine to a large extent what you do, and how you feel. If you believe you are a failure you will feel a certain way, and if you believe yourself a winner you will feel a different way. But you are not a prisoner of these characteristics. Many, but not all, of them can be changed, and you still have options. You can strengthen your associations where you want to or challenge them. But if you think of yourself as a victim—a helpless recipient of evil heaped on you by your parents, society, your genes, bad luck, or God Himself—you become paralyzed, unable to act, unable to imagine a better way of living for yourself.

God did not design you for hopelessness. Besides the identities already mentioned, God created you for a specific reason. He can take who you are right now and give you meaning and purpose.

Remember that shame is believing that you are not what you should be, or worse, believing that you are what you find despicable and don't want to be. To get out of shame, then, you need a firm grasp of who you really are from God's point of view. Some of His design is the same for all of His children. The details, though, are unique to each person.

If you know who you are according to God's plan, just like Jesus you don't have to be dependent on what other people think. You won't have to prove anything to yourself or to anybody else. You can be confident that as you submit yourself to what God wants you to do and be that He will bring to pass the purpose He has for you.

So what might this real you be like? Make a list of who the Bible says you are in Christ. What follows is a partial list. Add as many descriptions to the list as you can. If you want more than you can think of yourself, search the Internet for "who I am in Christ", and a dozen or so sites will supply you with even longer lists.

Redeemed—Colossians 1:14
Son or daughter of the King—2 Corinthians 6:18
Loved—Ephesians 3:18-19
Holy one (saint)—Romans 12:1
Friend of Jesus—John 15:15
Disciple of Christ—John 13:35
Light of the world—Matthew 5:14-16
Salt of the earth—Matthew 5:13
Foreknown—Romans 8:29
Predestined to be like God's son—Romans 8:29
More than conqueror—Romans 8:37-39
Chosen—John 15:16
Priest—1 Peter 2:9
A sheep of God's pasture—Psalm 23
Born anew—1 Peter 1:23
Temple of the Holy Spirit—1 Corinthians 6:19
Minister of reconciliation—2 Corinthians 5:18-20
God's workmanship—Ephesians 2:10
New creation—2 Corinthians 5:17

Notice that there is no shame in any of these descriptions. Thank God for who you are in Christ.

Write out the list, highlighting those elements that seem contradictory to how you see yourself. Stick that list on your bathroom mirror and go over it every day, or several times a day. If you don't see yourself like God sees you in some aspect, you have identified an area where the Holy Spirit needs to work in you. You really are who God says you are. Ask the Lord to work the truth into your life and make you fit these descriptions.

Since God says that he answers prayer which is according to his will, start by assuming that he will answer your prayer. Begin acting in accordance with who you really are instead of acting as you have always acted. If God says you are the salt of the earth, act like it. What would you do (or not do) if you were really the temple of the Holy Spirit? This is a matter of faith in what God says. If he says you are, assume that you are, whether you feel it or not, and start "playing the part." I don't mean that you should become obnoxious and lord it over others because you are a daughter of the King. But you could treat yourself with respect and expect that others will do the same.

Your acting will not change you. Remember we concluded that we can't get rid of our own shame, and the world certainly doesn't need any more hypocrites running around. Our healing has to be the work of the Holy Spirit in us. What the changed way of acting does is to reinforce your willingness to change. It helps you remember that you are asking for the Spirit to do a work of grace in you. It is stepping out on faith to be what God wants you to be. This may seem a bit like walking on water, but remember that Peter could do it when Jesus invited him to come.

The Lord used this very method to get me out of the isolation that shame imposed on my life, even though at the time I couldn't have described the process very well.

After I had been loved into the Kingdom by a group of Christian college students, they continued to help me overcome my shame by accepting me as a friend. I was also learning to trust the Lord more and look for what He might want to do in my life.

One day I read 2 Timothy 1:7 and it impressed me deeply. It says, "God did not give us a spirit of timidity, but a spirit of power, of love and of self-discipline." Sometimes "timidity" is translated as "fear". I knew that I had an attitude of fear and timidity. I was afraid of everybody, of every social situation. I was isolating myself from social contact because I "always" was shamed by others. It was as though I had built a wall around myself, about six feet high and as thick as the walls of a castle. There were battlements, just in case.

But I could see by this verse that God had not given me this attitude of fear. I decided that if God hadn't given it to me, I didn't want it, and I wasn't going to give in to it any more. But what could I put in its place? The verse says, "a spirit of power, of love and of self-discipline."

I didn't feel any of that, but I decided that if I had in theory received such a spirit (the Holy Spirit is like that), then perhaps I should start acting as though it were true and give the Spirit a chance, anyway. So when I had opportunities to relate to people I started asking myself what I would do if I felt love instead of the fear I really felt. Then I needed power and self-control in order to force myself to do it! To my complete surprise, it seemed to work. People weren't rejecting me. Little by little I started having friends, a complete novelty for me. I started taking down the wall, stone by stone. Little by little the fear fell away.

A few months later I got a note saying to report to the head of the Department of Chemistry. Generally a note like that means one is in deep trouble. A bit nervously I went to see him. He courteously invited me to sit down, and then said that in a faculty meeting that morning they had been talking about me. They had all noted that I had changed a lot recently, that I was much freer, much happier. They wanted to know what had happened to me.

Five decades later, I still have moments when shame gets hold of me. Habits die hard! Sometimes I want to hide behind my wall again and not see anyone. But now my normal pattern is to relax and be with people. I can now choose to love my neighbor. Before, that was not an option.

Everybody's story is different, and I am not suggesting that the path I took is normative for everyone. But there are elements of my story that may help others that want to be free. Perhaps your shame doesn't produce specifically the need for power, love and self-control. Perhaps you need to focus on the fact that you are beloved, or that you are royalty as the son or daughter of the King, or that you have been chosen, or that you are the temple of the Holy Spirit. Concentrate day after day on "living out" your true identity by acting in accordance with that identity.

Our enemy, the devil, loves to have us tied up in shame. Inform him that he is not welcome in your life with his lies about how unworthy you are. Show him who you are in Christ, and command him to leave you alone. If you are not accustomed to resisting the enemy, you may feel like twenty kinds of a fool doing this, but it really helps to declare your resistance out loud. Go somewhere where people can't hear you if you need to.

Shame is a habit, and most habits take a while to change, so keep practicing. Raise your head. Lay down the shame at Jesus' feet.

Going deeper

If identifying with Jesus as he took your shame and living out who you have become in Christ does not produce freedom even after allowing time for your habits to change, you may need to go deeper into how you came to be shamed.

It is not good to dwell in the past, or to ruminate on all of the rotten things that people have done to us over the years. All sorts of undesirable consequences lie down that road. Also, an understanding of why you are the way you are, in and of itself, does not produce change or healing. Nevertheless when you understand how your past influences your present you have the possibility of dealing with it and obtaining what some have called healing of emotional hurts.

So how can you come to that sort of understanding? The easiest way is to ask someone who knows you perfectly and who has been with you throughout your life: the Holy Spirit. He searches us and knows us completely, to the point where it can be scary to contemplate what would be an invasion of privacy if someone else were doing it. He even knows the filth that we don't want to admit even to ourselves.

In writing Psalm 139, David marvels at the profound knowledge that God has of him, but he also says he wants to get away from Him. When he acknowledges that God knows everything about his past and present, he says, "Where can I go from your Spirit? Where can I flee from your presence?" It can inspire fear to realize that someone knows us so deeply, even though we accept the theory that this person loves us. In Psalm 19 David asks God to free him from his hidden faults. We can't understand ourselves, but God understands better than we do, and he examines us freely.

Ask the Holy Spirit to fill you up, search you over, and help you understand your own story. Ask as King David did for the Lord to search and try him. Then just wait to see what happens. Don't try digging around through your insides to see what you can find. Memories and understanding will come to you, most likely when you least expect them—when you are waiting for a bus or washing dishes or caught in traffic or even sick in bed. You won't get everything at once. The Spirit knows us and knows how much we can take, so he supplies one or two things at a time, and then when we have dealt with them he will bring up something more.

More than ten years after my initial experience of healing of shame the Lord started working on me again. I had noticed that there were still many occasions when I would fall back into the old patterns, and I asked the Lord to show me why that happened and help me out of the hole. One memory at a time, I started connecting the dots between the past and the present, realizing things that should have been obvious, but which hadn't been so to me. The thoughts came in so many varied ways that it would be impossible to even catalogue them. Sometimes there would be a remark from a friend. At other times, a passage in a book would hit me hard. I remember one specific time when I was riding a city bus which was taking a very long time to work its way through traffic. I began to realize that in my head I had been "humming" the same tune over and over for nearly half an hour without realizing it. It was a tune I hadn't sung for ages, and I couldn't remember all the words. As I thought more about the tune, the words slowly came back to me, and most surprisingly they were a direct message from the Lord about something I needed to deal with in my past. This kind of revelation went on at a rate of two or three memories a week for about three months, and then it stopped.

Memories and understanding are not enough, though. You need to process what you discover. Since shame is an emotional reaction, the emotions that are associated with your memories are important. You need to allow yourself to feel again the hurt, anger, sadness, and discouragement that you felt when the event occurred, but without wallowing in this pain or feeling sorry for yourself.

OK, so now you have the memories and the understanding of how they have affected you, and you can feel deeply the hurt. That is a great recipe for becoming angry or embittered, if you're not that way already. Therefore the next step of forgiving the people that did it is of extreme importance.

Does that make you bristle and think that they don't deserve forgiveness? Of course they don't. You don't forgive them because they deserve it, but because Jesus said to do it and because if you don't you continue to be influenced by the experiences. You don't forgive as a favor to the offending person, who may never even know he has been forgiven. You forgive out of obedience to Christ and so you can live in peace.

There is a lot of misunderstanding about what it means to forgive. Whole books have been written on the subject. A basic guideline is Ephesians 4:32, which says that we should forgive one another as God in Christ has forgiven us. What happens when God forgives us?

First, there has been an offense, a real offense. God doesn't forgive us by making excuses for us, pretending that it wasn't really important. When we then forgive others, it doesn't mean that we have to minimize the hurt and the other person's responsibility. If you can find a good excuse for their behavior, perhaps you should excuse them, but forgiveness involves something wrong having been done.

Sometimes it helps to write out a balance sheet for people who have been important in your life. It is very probable that you have informal balance sheets in your head anyway. Nobody is all good or all bad, so probably the people who have most hurt you have also contributed something good to your life.

For each person, draw a line down the middle of a piece of paper. On one side list the positive things that the person has done. On the other side list the negative things. Then try putting a value on each item, using dollars (or euros, or whatever you are used to). For instance you might credit your dad with $20,000 for having provided you with a good education, but you might charge him with a similar amount for never having had time to spend with you. Take your time and be thorough.

When you have evaluated each item, add them up and get a balance of how much that person "owes" you (or how much you owe them, in case you had forgotten about the positive things). Set the sheet aside for the next step.

Second, when God forgives us in Christ he sees that the debt has been paid by Christ on the cross. Jesus died for all of us. Some people haven't yet appropriated that sacrifice for themselves, but it is there waiting for them if they so choose. That means sins committed against you have been covered, even those committed by unbelievers. You have the option of deciding to accept that and consider that the price has been paid for those sins, or not.

Jesus said that what we forgive on earth will be forgiven in heaven, and what we don't forgive will remain (Matthew 18:18). Essentially this gives you the option to go before the Lord and declare whether you will press charges against the other person.

If you say you want to press charges, God says "Vengeance is mine, I will repay" (Romans 12:19). When the offending person comes before the Lord, that offense will be on his record. If the other person is a Christian, of course, he will have the very best lawyer standing right there by the judge (I John 2:1).

If you tell the Lord you won't press charges, he will wipe the slate clean of that offense. You can't forgive what has been done against me, but you can choose to remove the sin against you from the record. What do you want to do?

Before you answer that question, read the story of the unforgiving servant that follows on from the verse we saw before in Matthew 18. After describing the wrath of the King whose servant wouldn't forgive a fellow servant after he himself had been forgiven by the King, Jesus says that the King will turn that servant over to the torturers. Then he adds that his Father will do the same with everyone who will not forgive his brother from his heart (Matthew 18:34-35).

He isn't talking about torture in hell after death, but rather the torture that unforgiving people feel here on earth. Resentment and anger can eat you up emotionally and even physically. If someone has shamed you and you refuse to forgive, you may continue with your shame.

To put it another way, if you don't forgive, you give the offending person the power to continue to hurt you. They may have ruined part of your life, but if you choose to hang on to the hurt and shame, they can ruin the rest of your life also. If you set them free, you can be free, too.

So if you decide it is in your best interest to forgive the person, take the balance sheet and write in big, colorful letters across it "PAID IN FULL" and sign it.

Now the deal with a bill that has been paid is that you can no longer collect on it. We have so many ways of collecting for past hurts: cold silence, hurtful remarks, gossip, or whatever. Once you sign that paper, you can't do that anymore. It is not necessary (or in some cases even advisable) to tell the person he has been forgiven, but your behavior toward him may have to change. Forgiveness does not mean giving the person permission to hurt you again. It just wipes out the past debt.

The *third* aspect of God's forgiveness of us in Christ is that he doesn't ruminate on our sins. He doesn't continually go over them, and even says that he forgets them (Hebrews 8:12).

Forgetting is hard, since if you try to forget you are automatically thinking about the matter and keeping the memory alive. It may not be possible to keep the thoughts from coming into your head, but you do have the option of thinking about something else instead when you catch your mind going back to the matter. It doesn't work to try to blank out your mind. Try not thinking about green elephants. The more you try just blotting out green elephants, the more you think of them. It is better to think an alternate thought, such as normal-colored elephants, or what to fix for supper.

In forgiveness, perhaps the best alternate thought is how much you have been forgiven, or how good Jesus is to you. Each time you are tempted to think how much that person has wronged you, remind yourself of how gracious Jesus has been with you. If you keep that up, sooner or later you won't be thinking about the offense much at all, and you may even forget, even something important.

The *fourth* aspect of God's forgiveness is that he actively works for good for those he has forgiven. Jesus says to love our enemies (and brothers and neighbors and non-friends) and pray for them that despitefully use us. Pray for them in such a way that they would be happy if they heard you. Sometimes it may not be advisable to have further contact with the person, especially in the case of outright abuse, but you can ask for the Lord's blessing on them, and that if they are not Christ-followers that they could come to faith.

Having forgiven, ask the Lord to take away the habit of shame from your life, fill you up with the Holy Spirit, and help you to live in power, love, and self-control.

Some people may find this program very difficult to do all by themselves. If you have difficulty with it, you may want to find someone you can trust with whom you can talk about it. There are many things to consider before involving other people in our private struggles, so we'll deal with that in the next chapter.

Questions for reflection:

1. How have you responded to Jesus' taking on himself your guilt and shame?
2. What aspects of the shame you have felt are due to your own actions and should be dealt with as guilt?
3. Amplify the list of who you are in Christ from your own searching of the Bible, or from Internet sites. With which of the descriptions do you identify the best? Do you have difficulty seeing yourself as God sees you in regard to any of the descriptions? Why is this aspect of who you really are so difficult for you to realize? Where did this difficulty

come from? What can you do to make this description true of you?

4. Try asking the Holy Spirit to search you over to find places that need to be healed. What happens when you do that?

5. Are there any people that are difficult for you to forgive? Who are they, and what have they done? What are the consequences in your life of not forgiving them? Make up a balance sheet for each of them and see what the score is. Will you press charges against them?

CHAPTER 7 **Healing in Community**

Shame is learned in a social context, with other people. Because of this, it separates us from others. Adam and Eve hid from God, and from one another. Cain was forced away from society. Isolation is a key problem for shame-prone people. It should not come as a surprise, then, that other people can be very important in healing us of shame. Complete healing from shame happens in community.

All of those who write about shame, whether they write from a Christian or a secular viewpoint, are in agreement that an essential step in seeking freedom from shame is opening yourself up and allowing someone else to know you. You need others to understand you, and to accept and love you, perhaps in spite of what they know about you. The disease is social, and so is the remedy. A book—such as this one, for example—can be of help (and I hope it will be) but it isn't sufficient, because it is impersonal. You need a healing community which can show you grace in a way you can see and appreciate.

If you hide from others you may avoid feeling some of the pain of shame, but you can't get rid of it unless you stop hiding. First you have to stop hiding from yourself and from God, as we discussed in the last chapter. Many people will have trouble putting the last chapter into practice all by themselves, and others will find that besides the love and acceptance of Jesus they need a flesh-and-blood person at their side. In fact, healing from shame implies that your relationships with other humans will change, and that you will be freer to interact with them. So you have to take the step of starting to dismantle whatever kind of protective wall you have made for yourself.

Sharing honestly how you feel with someone you trust should help get you out of your isolation. You need to see yourself reflected in the eyes of at least one person who does not shame you. The experience of being accepted— without reference to whether you deserve it or not— is the beginning of the end for your feeling of being unacceptable.

You need to let others inspect the shame itself. In there, you may be hiding your inner feelings of humiliation, insufficiency, and low self-esteem. But shame recognized and exposed for what it is can more easily be transformed into guilt or even absolved. If you have sinned and are trapped in shame, it is hard to repent, because you are preoccupied with covering up the sin. If you have not sinned but still feel shame, you need relief from that interior voice that accuses you. But you have to open up in order for others to help with this.

This probably sounds very, very scary. You may have had other people who knew your secrets turn on you and use what they knew against you, and you are afraid it will happen again. Perhaps your core fears or weaknesses could inspire disgust or ridicule or condemnation on the part of those you might tell about them. You could end up losing the only friends you thought you had if they were to react badly to knowing you more deeply. What if they tell everyone about you? The last thing you need is to be shamed even more. My husband tells a horror story from his high school years about confiding to a friend some of his struggles to live a Christian life. The "friend" exaggerated what he heard out of all proportion and spread ugly rumors about him.

These are real dangers, so you need to choose very carefully with whom you share. You need your capacity for trust restored, not obliterated. Here are some guidelines for choosing an individual with whom to share.

1. You need to choose a mature counselor, preferably of the same sex, who will listen and understand without trying to impose his or her opinions on you.

2. If you have ever heard the person gossip about others, it would be better to choose someone else. If they have done it to others, they may do it to you.

3. Unless you both agree that the relationship will be mutual help (which I will talk about shortly), you should be sure to choose someone who doesn't show a lot of signs of suffering from shame. Check them out with the characteristics described in previous chapters of this book. Some shame-prone people love to counsel others because it makes them feel superior. If listening to you is helping to puff up their ego and fulfill their needs for self-esteem, their needs may lead them to further shame you. If someone seems to have difficulty relating to others unless they are helping them, it would be better to choose someone else.

4. Family members are not a good choice because they are too close to you. They may think they already know more about you than you yourself do, so it may be hard to share what you really think and feel. You may have to continue to live with them, and they may even have participated in the shaming process. Especially your closest relatives— father, mother, brother, sister, husband, or wife—are not good choices.

5. It may be advisable to do this with a professional therapist, an expert who has studied how to help.

Ministering to one another in a group

You've just read the subheading for this section, and I can practically hear you screaming, *"Whoa!* I don't even know *one* person I would be comfortable sharing my life with, and already you're talking about a *group! Get real!"* As strange as it may seem, it may actually be easier to get together a group than to establish a one-on-one relationship with someone for this purpose. The group experience also tends to be less intense, in case that is a problem for you.

The first time I ever consciously led a group which helped people deal with their shame, it was an accident. I had offered in a church to lead a group for women who had family members with addictions, such as alcohol, drugs, and gambling. At the first meeting 24 ladies showed up, and although some dropped out after a while, a dozen or so continued meeting weekly for over a year. As we dealt with the dynamics of dysfunctional families the ladies began sharing their experiences and learned to help one another. They slowly began to lower their barriers. As they knew each other better and better, the focus of the group shifted from how to manage (or rather stop trying to manage) their wayward relatives to managing their own habits of thinking that were keeping them bound in shame.

Sometime later, another group of women, many of whom were in ministry, wanted some help with their tendency to be constantly helping others. Some of them were really worn out with feeling that they had to meet everyone's needs, so we called ourselves "The Marthas", in reference to the friend of Jesus whom He described as "anxious and troubled about many things". We established this as a "mutual ministry" group, especially since being a helper is a temptation for me also. The group continued to meet for three or four years, and served as a support group besides helping some people out of the shame which was motivating them to over-help.

A pastor's wife in another church asked me to start a group for the ladies in her church who were troubled by depression. There were lots of them. For a majority of them, the main underlying problem stoking their depression was shame. Gradually the women in the group began understanding their own difficulties and were able to minister to each other the acceptance and support they needed to lift their heads and get on with their lives. This group lasted nearly a year.

These three examples of groups got started not by suggesting that people needed to deal with shame, but rather with some problem that could be a result of shame or which could produce a lot of shame. Shame is a fairly predictable problem in families with addictions. It is also a common reason behind depression and compulsive helping. Remember that people with shame don't want to publicize that fact, and may not want to attend a group that is advertised as dealing with shame. So start a group that focuses on something which could be related to shame: burnout, anger, timidity or compulsive shopping.

The three examples above are notably all of women. The men are harder to get together. One man suggested that there would never be shame groups for men because the men would be too ashamed to come. That is true, but the same ploy of announcing a related but non-shameful theme for the group will work. Men will come to a group to help them with burnout because of overwork. I've done this. Burnout is an acceptable problem because it sounds very noble to have worked so hard.

If you are a Christian, a group of fellow believers who practice accepting one another is an exceptionally good place to look for healing from shame, even if that wasn't specifically the original purpose of the group.

A model for what is needed can be found in the relationship between Jesus and his disciples at the Last Supper. Jesus demonstrates the depth of his acceptance and love of his followers by washing their feet. This shows humility on Jesus' part, but also on the part of the disciples. Peter didn't want to let him do it, but finally gave in and accepted. It requires humility to let someone wash your feet (even figuratively), especially if you respect the person who washes and want them to respect you.

Jesus says that we should wash each other's feet. Although there are groups that do this literally and physically, usually the phrase is taken figuratively to mean that we help each other deal with the dirt in our lives. According to Jesus, it should be reciprocal, "Now that I, your Lord and Teacher, have washed your feet, you also should wash one another's feet. I have set you an example that you should do as I have done for you" (John 13:14-15). Everyone washes. Everyone is washed. You have to let others see into the dirty corners of your life and help clean you up. This is not comfortable, whether you wash or whether you are washed.

In another context, Jesus warned of the danger of seeing the speck in someone else's eye and ignoring the beam in your own (Mathew 7:3-5). If you have shame in your own life and don't take care of it before you try to help someone else, you can't help them. So it is important that the activity be reciprocal, especially in the matter of shame. There is nobody perfect here, nobody without needs, nobody superior to everyone else. The first step in a profound change could be that someone who knows you as you really are accepts you, loves you, and even admires you.

Pastors first

I once was privileged to attend a meeting of Spanish evangelical pastors who were talking about the problems they saw in their churches. They identified authoritarianism, egotism, pride, and excessive control, and underneath all of that they saw fear and insecurity. Many of them said they felt incapable of receiving the grace of God for themselves and had a need to realize their own identity in Christ. Most important, they perceived the general need of inner healing among the leadership of the Church.

You will recognize that the problems the pastors saw are effects of shame. The Spanish pastors are not the only ones to be affected, just the honest ones I happened to hear that day. This is a general problem throughout the Church. It is urgent that pastors and elders be freed from their shame so that they can minister life, not death, to their congregations and the unbelievers in their area.

When shame-prone people minister in the Church, the result is that shame is propagated to others. The pastor of a church who is constantly in a position of guiding his people both by word and example needs to be healthy to the core. The emotional atmosphere of any organization, including the church, is usually established from the top down. If the pastor is healthy and his interactions with others are healthy, he can be an instrument for healing for his congregation. If not, he is in a position to do a great deal of harm to people who trust him to lead them rightly.

One would hope that the calling and the empowering of the Lord would automatically take care of any shame present. Grace is always sufficient, but many times the needed treatment is not applied. The doctrine of many churches supposes that all of the promises of God are realized in our lives automatically when we receive Christ as our Savior, so healing from old emotional damage is never sought after. In some cases the shame is well hidden under a lot of ability and success in ministry, and doesn't surface until much later when there may be more stress.

However it may be, it is difficult for a pastor to ask for help. Many assume that when one gets to be a pastor he must already have everything he needs. Some just don't have anyone in whom they can confide. It seems inappropriate to go to someone in the congregation. The denominational supervisor could be a dangerous confidant since he might take away the pastorate. Other pastors in the region may be seen as competitors, not companions. They may also be afraid that someone might find out they have a weakness, which might be exploited. So the needed help doesn't arrive.

Unless the denomination has a really good system of putting potential pastors "under care" by people who really know how to help, it is entirely possible to begin ministry loaded down with a lot of hurt and shame. In this state they are expected to minister to sheep which have the same problems. They would like to help, but they cannot administer healing that they themselves have not received. It also often happens that in trying to help they do more damage.

It is not surprising that if both the pastor and the congregation are loaded down with shame, sooner or later the defenses that they normally use to protect themselves from the pain of shame will start to come out and affect relationships within the congregation. A lot of congregational conflict which is described as "personality differences" is actually due to this effect.

The emotional and spiritual health of a pastor will be severely tested. Our enemy will regularly supply situations where a pastor will feel attacked, inadequate, rejected, treated with apathy or looked down upon. It is important that his sense of identity and authority not be based on the approval and recognition by others. Depending on human approval makes anyone vulnerable to shame, because that approval may disappear at any moment. Jesus is our model for ministry. He did not give in to all the demands of his followers, sometimes seriously disappointing them. The apostle Paul dealt with this issue in Galatians

1:10 where he says that if he were still trying to please people he would not be a servant of Christ.

So pastors need to be sure they have dealt with their shame. Forming a group with other regional pastors may be one way of going at it. There are also various organizations that minister to ministers.

If you are a pastor, check these things out.

Group essentials

In order to avoid the obvious dangers of opening yourself up in a group, there must be some understanding among the members about what can and can't be done. There must be commitment between the people in the group, that they will attend the meetings, that they will be genuine with each other, and especially that they will keep what is said within the group. What each person shares in the group belongs to that person, and cannot be shared with anyone outside the group (no, not even spouses!). This is very important since it allows security in sharing. Those who don't want to keep the secrets of others should not be in the group. Addiction to gossip is a bondage that should keep a potential member out. They need to get help elsewhere first to avoid putting the people in the group at risk of further shame.

This begins to sound a bit formal, and probably it should be so. In our ordinary informal contacts we don't reach a level of confidence that leads to disclosure. We need some commitment in order to feel secure.

Talking about your feelings of shame can be a help toward freedom, but it is important that the focus of the group not be on this process but on Jesus. He is the healer who has been wounded by shame and who can free us. The group must not degenerate into collective wallowing in shame, but rather as we receive confessions we should pray for one another that we may be healed (James 5:14-16).

Where can you find a group like that? Probably nowhere. They don't exist if people don't make the effort to form them. The Church, among brothers and sisters, should be a good place to start to look for others with the same desire to get out of shame, or some other related difficulty. One person who feels the need personally or recognizes that others may have that need could start organizing a group. I started a group for pastors' wives and women missionaries, for example, as I saw that there were people who needed it. Membership in the group was by invitation only.

Someone needs to coordinate the group, organizing the meeting place, collecting news from people who are absent, keeping the discussion on target, and closing on time. But the coordinator needs to come with the attitude of being just one more shamed person in the struggle. Leaders who approach the group wanting to solve all of everyone's problems communicate that they are superior to the others in the group, making the others inferior, a position of shame. Leaders who have been successful at dealing with most of their shame are perhaps most likely to be of help, since they can understand what the others are going through.

There is no fixed rule about what to do in the group, though it should be obvious that the most important activity is to pray for one another. In James 5:16 we are told, "confess your sins to each other and pray for each other so that you may be healed. The prayer of a righteous man is powerful and effective." In confessing our sin, we should also confess our shame. Each person needs the work of the Spirit, and the members of the group can agree to ask for this.

Getting started may seem a bit awkward, though after relationships have been established things seem more natural. One way to get started would be to walk through the chapters of this book together. The reflection questions at the end of each chapter would be good springboards for discussion.

The group is a good place to try to acquire a balanced self-concept. In Romans 12:3 we are told that we ought to think of ourselves with sober judgment. This is hard for anyone to do all alone, but if you are shame-prone it may be doubly hard. Having the input of people who know and accept you is a valuable aid to sorting out your good and bad points. Nobody is all good or all bad, but shame-prone people notoriously have a skewed picture of themselves. Since your emotional experience of shame is based on what you believe you are, getting this clearer in your mind can be very helpful. You need to know that a person who has been accepted in the Beloved, as you have, does not have to be perfect in order to be acceptable.

The group can also help by celebrating any reasons the members might have for healthy satisfaction with themselves. There is good pride, which is a satisfaction, especially about something that you or someone with whom you identify has done. This is not the same as boastfulness, the bad pride that accompanies shame, that which expresses itself in arrogance or self-exaltation, that which says, "I can control you," or "I know more than you do," or "I am better than you are." It is OK to be happy with who God made you to be and dance happily a bit when something you do turns out well.

Some people have found that the *Twelve Steps* developed by Alcoholics Anonymous have been an excellent guide to group work. John Bradshaw, in his excellent book, *Healing the Shame that Binds You*, presents a detailed for dealing with shame program based on this system. The Steps are completely compatible with good Christian faith and practice, having been developed by Christian men to deal with alcoholism.

Some notes on group dynamics

There is a popular idea that conversation consists of talking. Talking is only half of a conversation, though. Someone has to listen. You will appreciate this if you are sharing something that is important to you and find others in the group looking out the window, looking for something in a book, talking to someone else, seeming to want to speak themselves, or even interrupting you. When people do that to me, I want to just stop talking, since it seems that nobody wants to listen to me.

Listening well is an integral part of helping someone else combat shame. A powerful way to shame people is to treat them with apathy, ignore what they say, or make them feel like a thing, a case, instead of a person. Since the main purpose of getting together is to combat shame, obviously showing interest and a desire to understand are top priority.

While someone is sharing, the others should be thinking about what is said, not about what they themselves will say the next time there is a chance for them to speak. It helps the speaker if from time to time the audience shows signs of listening and understanding, such as nodding or making brief comments (which do not take the turn away from the speaker). Visual contact is important, too. You may not have observed this before, but we have a tendency to look to the side while we talk, then look at another person when we are passing them the conversational ball. Check it out next time you are having a conversation with someone. Looking at someone communicates that you want him or her to talk. Exaggerated staring could be interpreted as impolite, but friendly looks encourage talking.

It is difficult to listen well if you want to direct the conversation or control the situation, so it is important to lay aside your agenda in favor of the ideas the other person is expressing. This is especially important if you tend to relieve the pain of your own shame by helping others. It will be a temptation for you to want to supply the answer to each and every problem the other people bring up. If you do this you will give the impression that you think you know how best to live and that you have the right to prescribe for others. If that is your way of doing things, practice keeping your mouth shut and see how it goes. The best solution for a problem will probably be one that the person who has it discovers for him—or herself.

Keeping this in mind, those who have the responsibility to coordinate a group should be people who have dealt sufficiently with their own shame so that they will not feel the need to impose their ideas on others. Anyone who denies having had to struggle with shame or who declares themselves completely free of it is not the indicated leader of such a group. If those in the group are mature Christians, it is possible that they don't need a leader. If they understand well what they need to do, they can just help one another.

It is important to avoid pressuring people to open themselves up when they don't do so spontaneously. You need to be free to be who you really are, and to talk about yourself when and how you want. When you feel understood after sharing a little, you may want to open up more, but there is no automatic way of producing this, and most attempts to force people to be more open usually make people clam up instead. Some will share more freely than others. It is easier to share when you have a good concept of yourself, but many shame-prone people do not have that good concept.

Men especially have difficulties expressing their feelings, since they usually don't have the custom of doing so. They may use silence to distance themselves from the discussion, and may intellectualize the topic being discussed so it won't get too personal. It is very important not to push them nor take away their protection. If there is a barrier, it is there for a reason. If you don't know the reason, don't tear it down, or you may hurt the person.

Some people suggest that the groups should have a mixture of men and women so that people will receive affirmation from both sexes. My observations lead me to the opposite conclusion. The level of intimacy that can be reached in a group may be quite deep, and could lead to temptations that it would be best to avoid altogether.

Although the group may ask for a certain amount of accountability, be careful about confrontation. The person who suffers from a lot of shame may react with fury if his inconsistencies, failures, sins and suchlike are brought out into the open by someone else. Instead of saying that someone is wrong, for example, it might be better to say that certain strategies or attitudes "aren't helping you very much". Pray for one another that you may be healed, and respect the fact that the Holy Spirit works at different speeds in different people.

Avoid wallowing in dirt. Say what needs to be said for others to understand where you are coming from, but don't go into unnecessary details, especially about your own sins or those that others have committed against you. There is a tendency, in both religious and secular circles, toward the practice of confessing everything publicly. Sometimes it seems like people want to bring out the worst filth possible in order to impress or move others. That is not the purpose of the exercise. The Bible warns us in Proverbs 18:2, "A fool finds no pleasure in understanding but delights in airing his own opinions." Let's not be fools, but work toward understanding.

If everyone is in the same process, there will be times when understanding doesn't necessarily come from how another person has described his or her situation, but rather from having experienced something similar. This can rapidly produce a sense of community in the group, but be careful about taking for granted that you understand what someone is saying when you haven't listened enough to hear the whole story. Just as you think you understand, some important factor you hadn't known about can change the whole story. It is a serious error to declare that you understand someone else without having taken the trouble to listen to what he is saying.

In the same way, when someone tells a story similar to one of yours, resist the temptation to jump in with your story. This will not make people feel understood. Instead they may feel that you are in competition with them and that you think your story is better than theirs. It was their turn to talk, so let them talk. Errors of this kind can build barriers, and may make it difficult for that person to feel like sharing again.

Going on from there

The help of the group may be valuable for some time. The Lord had me protected in a caring group for a couple of years before I had to get into situations which would have been overwhelming before. Most of the groups with which I have been involved have lasted no more than a couple of years. The people have dealt with what they needed to deal with, and it was time to move on.

One surprise that you may encounter is the reaction of another group, your family, to the change in you. Families have a tendency to want to stay the same as always, and when one member starts to change that changes the relationships between everyone. Even when the changes are for the better, they may introduce tension into the family system. The members of the family want everything to go on like it was, even when that way of being was uncomfortable. It was, well, familiar.

There may be resistance, then, on the part of your relatives and friends, people you had hoped would be happy about your new way of being. It can be a shock to find that they oppose your acting in liberty, and perhaps even try to sabotage it. I have seen families of dieters push chocolate cake at them, families of drug users urge the former addict to associate with his old friends, and families of former smokers telling them one cigarette won't hurt them. Don't get sidetracked if your family does this. Continue with what God is doing in your life. Keep on loving your family and remember that this change was something you decided to do, not something they agreed to. Perhaps in a little while they may want to do something similar, too.

As you are in the process of being healed of shame you can help yourself and others at the same time by sharing what the Lord is doing in your life. Even though it is not acceptable to share the stories of other people in you group, you can tell your own story. If you are being healed of shame, your testimony can be used by God to help others, keeping in mind the humility needed and avoiding the pitfalls of trying to take charge of other people's lives.

Having been rejected in the past does not take away the possibility of ministering to others. What you were does not dictate what you will be. Your past is not your destiny. In Psalm 118:22-23 we read, "The stone the builders rejected has become the capstone; the Lord has done this, and it is marvelous in our eyes." Don't let past rejections form your ideas of what the Lord could or could not do with you in the present or in the future.

Be careful, though, how you apply to other people what you are learning about shame. As you understand the concept and recognize the symptoms in yourself, you will start to see what appears to be shame in other people's lives. Recognizing that does not give you a license to try to fix them.

First of all, you may be interpreting wrongly what you see. Acting on your false assumptions could do a lot of damage. Second, remember that if they have not asked you for help, you shame them further by offering it. That is true no matter how clearly you can see what their problem is. And the more you want to be the one to help and the more you are convinced that you are the one to do it, the more you need to suspect that you still haven't gotten over your own need to dominate and control. Pray for them and offer them appreciation and acceptance. Then be sure you've gotten the beam out of your own eye before trying to help them. When you have gotten to the point where you really *don't* want to give them a hand, God may give you your golden opportunity to do just that.

Questions for reflection:

1. When you think about letting someone else know about the shame you feel, what is your emotional reaction? What logical arguments can you find against doing such a thing? Are they valid? What would it cost you to open your heart to someone you trusted? Would it be worth it, really? If the desired result is that you can walk with your head held high, wouldn't it be better just to practice doing that?

2. If you were to open up to someone, what kind of person would that have to be? Do you know anyone like that? Where might you find someone?

3. How can you find out if there are other people you know who want to get free from shame? Where would you look? Could you form a group to help with this? What kind of group would it be?

CHAPTER 8 **Who's in Charge Here?**

The first question the optometrist asked when I said I wanted contact lenses was, "How badly do you want them?" A variation of the question came up when I said in another context that I wanted to lose a lot of weight. The reason for the questions was that the projects would require some perseverance on my part and were not to be entered into lightly. I needed to be willing to confront difficulty and stick it out.

If you have read to this point either you are interested in getting rid of some shame in your own life, or you want to help other people do so. If you want to help, you need to make sure you are fairly shame-free yourself, as I have said before. So either way you'll need to apply the steps that have been outlined in previous chapters.

Therefore, you may be trying to change your habitual way of thinking about yourself. Shame is a habit. Habits change slowly, usually with careful consideration and effort. Are you willing to step up and take charge of this area of your life?

A young woman came to me one day with an unusual proposition. She wanted me to take charge of her emotional health. She said that she would do anything that I told her to do, so she was sure it would work out all right. She said that her doctor was in charge of her physical health, her husband was in charge of their financial situation and the discipline of their children, her pastor was in charge of her spiritual life, and she just needed me to make sure she remained emotionally healthy. I asked her what she herself was in charge of. She gleefully answered that with those arrangements she didn't have to do anything. She wasn't responsible for what happened to her.

Needless to say, I didn't accept the deal.

Other people can be of help, but in the end each person is responsible for his or her own life. You can choose how to react to what people have done to you. If you feel shame, you can choose how you will act in consequence. Shame does not condemn you to a life of bondage. Like Cain, you have the ability to choose between hiding and defending yourself or doing what you know you need to do. It is to your advantage to decide to stop thinking and acting like a shamed person.

This is a decision you will have to make not once but over and over again. It is not realistic to hope that patterns of thought, feelings, and action that have been developed over many years will change completely in a few minutes, however sincere your decision may be. You will not get rid of any shame because of knowing a great quantity of information about it. Neither will a fantastic spiritual experience solve all of your problems instantly. Sometimes changes may be dramatic, but in order to maintain them you need to discipline yourself to act in a way consistent with freedom. The favor and healing that God offers you is free, but it isn't cheap. It requires commitment and action on your part. Just reading this book will not fix the problem.

The process of getting free from shame will oblige you to learn new habits of thinking and acting. There will be advances and there will be times when you feel like you're back where you started. You may have to repeatedly reject the lies that come to your head automatically.

That having been said, the most responsible thing you can do for your life is to turn over the reins to Jesus. This is not a contradiction of what I said before. It is a commitment to living your life God's way. We all have a pattern of wanting to do things our own way instead of His way. Doing things your own way can lead to doing things that are hurtful to yourself and others, actions we often call sins. This of course produces guilt. Also the shame you are trying to get rid of probably came to you because some people went their own way. If you want to get rid of the shame you need to get onto a road that leads to better things.

Procedurally, turning the direction of your life over to the Lord is not hard. Jesus didn't stay dead. He rose again, and is alive and present with you all the time. So all you have to do to communicate with Him is start talking, just as with an ordinary human. Tell Him you're sorry you have been trying to run your own life, and thank Him for suffering and dying in order to take away your guilt and shame. Ask Him to come into your life, and tell Him that you want to do things His way now. In Revelation 3:20 Jesus promises that if anyone responds to His desire to have a relationship by asking Him in, He will come in. Maybe you will feel something. Maybe you won't. The important thing is to make the contract.

I said that this isn't hard procedurally, but for heavily shamed people it is sometimes difficult. For one thing, you lose some control over your life, which can seem like a threat. Just keep in mind to whom you are ceding control. Jesus is not going to shame you. He suffered and died to take away the shame. He is reliable, even though some of the people who claim to be His followers may not be.

If you have been defending yourself against the pain of shame by the strong method, you may also have difficulty admitting you have been wrong. This was a problem for me for a long time. I was willing to say I believed that all human beings sin and come short of what God wants us to be (Romans 3:23), but somehow I managed to make an exception in my own case. Once a guy in the Christian group I ran around with called everyone to leave for an event by saying, "Come on, sinners!" I actually responded with anger, saying that I wasn't one!

If that sounds like you, go as far as you can. Ask Jesus to come into your life and run the show, and to let you know if there is anything that needs to change. When He comes in, the Holy Spirit does, too, and the Spirit's job is to light up the dark places in our lives. He'll let you know, not cruelly like some other human might but rather in a way you can respond to, so you can work on fixing whatever it is.

If you have been defending yourself against shame by the weak method, please note that asking Jesus to be in control does not mean that you are acquiring a difficult taskmaster. He has not died for you in order to get work out of you. There will be work to do, but you are not to earn your relationship with Him that way. If you want to go along on some of His adventures, ask Him, and maybe He will let you hold some of the tools while He is working. He invites all those who are weary and burdened to come to Him because His yoke is easy and His burden is light (Matthew 11:28-30).

If you have been a perfectionist, do not try to clean up your life first before asking Jesus in. For one thing, you can't do it. You'll miss some spots, particularly the really deep dirt you probably don't even know about. Some folks who have tried to change all of their bad habits by themselves have noticed that while they are concentrating on one area, other habits they thought they had already corrected slip back to being like they were before. Let the Expert help you work on it.

There is one more step that is often difficult for shamed people. After you ask Jesus into your life you need to tell someone that you have become a Christ follower. Jesus said that whoever acknowledged Him before men, He would also acknowledge him before His Father in heaven. But whoever disowned Him before men, He would disown him before His Father in heaven. (Matthew 10:32-33).

This isn't just an arbitrary requirement. There are two very practical reasons why you need to do this. One is that it will make your decision firmer if someone else knows that you did it. The other reason you need to tell someone is that opening yourself up to another human being is one of the necessary steps for getting out of shame.

It will be easiest to do if you choose to tell someone you know will be really delighted that you have asked Jesus into your life. If you don't know anyone like that and you are afraid to tell your friends and family, find a stranger who seems friendly enough, someone you aren't likely to see ever again, and just tell them. Don't go into a lot of details in that case, unless they ask. Otherwise it would be too much information. Ask Jesus to give you an idea of someone to tell.

Once you have a relationship with Jesus, you can claim all of those descriptions in Chapter 6 about "who you are in Christ". This gives you some basic tools you need to work on shame. You will need more direction, though, if you want to do things God's way. You need to get yourself a Bible, or at least a New Testament, and start to read it. If you are new to this, start with the New Testament. God will speak to you through His word if you ask Him.

Talk to the Lord about what you read in the Bible, and ask Him to show you how it applies to your life. Tell Him about everything that concerns you, and ask Him to take care of it all. You don't necessarily need formal prayers, because this is a relationship. You can talk with Him as you would with a family member or your best friend.

You also need a relationship with other people who follow Jesus. Find some Christians and start associating with them for mutual support and community worship of the Savior you have in common.

The goal of this is for you to walk in freedom, so that when people want to shame you you can just shake it off and maybe even send them back a blessing. God wants to take away your desire to duck your head and hide. To describe Himself He says, "I am the Lord your God; . . . I broke the bars of your yoke and enabled you to walk with heads held high" (Leviticus 26:13). Or as David says in Psalm 3:3, "You are a shield around me, O Lord; you bestow glory on me and lift up my head."

Heads up!

About the author

Carolyn Kerr has a doctorate in clinical psychology and a master's degree in theology, from Fuller Theological Seminary and the Fuller Graduate School of Psychology. She has been in Christian ministry for 35 years in Costa Rica, California, and Spain. She and her husband have three children and eight grandchildren. They live in Valparaiso, Indiana, and Seville, Spain.

Bibliography

I have made no attempt to provide a complete bibliography on the subject of shame. Below are listed some books that you might find helpful for further investigation, including the works I have mentioned in the book.

Alcoholics Anonymous. *Twelve Steps and Twelve Traditions.* New York: Alcoholics Anonymous World Services, Inc., 1952, 1953.

Bradshaw, John. *Healing the Shame that Binds You.* Deerfield Beach, Florida: Health Communications, Inc., 1988.

Brown, Brené. *I Thought It Was Just Me (but it isn't): Telling the truth about perfectionism, inadequacy and power.* New York: Gotham Books, 2007.

Camus, Albert. *The Fall.* New York: Vintage Books, 1956.

Gottman, John. *The Relationship Cure.* New York: Three Rivers Press, 2001.

Eisenstadt, D., and M. R. Leippe. "The Self-Comparison Process and Self-Discrepant Feedback: Consequences of Learning You Are What You Thought You Were Not." *Journal of Personality and Social Psychology* 67 (1994): 611-626.

Joy, Donald. *Rebonding.* Waco, Texas: Word Books, 1986.

Joyner, Rick. *Epic Battles of the Last Days.* New Kensington, Pennsylvania: Whitaker House, 1995.

Joyner, Rick. *The Final Quest.* New Kensington, Pennsylvania: Whitaker House, 1996.

Kerr, Carolyn E. "Shame in Spain." *Evangelical Missions Quarterly,* 42, (2007): 358-364.

Kraft, Charles. *Two Hours to Freedom.* Grand Rapids: Chosen Books, 2010.

Lewis, Helen Block. *Shame and Guilt in Neurosis.* New York: International Universities Press, 1971.

Lewis, Michael. *Shame: The Exposed Self.* New York: The Free Press, 1992.

Niedenthal, P. M., J. P. Tangney, and I. Gavanski. "'If Only I Weren't' Versus 'If Only I Hadn't:' Distinguishing Shame and Guilt in Counterfactual Thinking." *Journal of Personality and Social Psychology,* 67 (1994): 585-595.

Powell, John. *Why Am I Afraid to Tell You Who I Am?* Niles, Illinois: Argus Communications, 1969.

Pulakos, Joan. "Family Environment and Shame: Is There a Relationship?" *Journal of Clinical Psychology* 52 (1996): 617-623.

Rohner, Ronald. "Parental Acceptance-Rejection: Theory, Methods, Cross-Cultural Evidence, and Implications." Internet Web site: http://vm.uconn.edu/~rohner/intropar.html. (2004)

Smedes, Lewis B. *Shame and Grace: Healing the Shame We Don't Deserve.* Grand Rapids: Zondervan, 1993.

Tangney, J. P., and R. L. Dearing. *Shame and Guilt.* New York: The Guilford Press, 2002.

Tangney, J. P. "Moral Affect: the Good, the Bad, and the Ugly." *Journal of Personality and Social Psychology* 61 (1991): 598-607.

Tangney, J. P., P. Wagner, C. Fletcher, and R. Gramzow, "Shamed into Anger? The Relation of Shame and Guilt to Anger and Self-Reported Aggression." *Journal of Personality and Social Psychology* 62 (1992): 669-675.

Ten Boom, Corrie, E. Sherrill, and J. Sherrill. *The Hiding Place.* Grand Rapids: Baker Book House, 1983.

Tournier, Paul. *Guilt and Grace.* New York: Harper and Row, 1962.

Tournier, Paul. *The Strong and the Weak.* Westminster John Knox, 1976.

Tournier, Paul. *The Healing of Persons.* Westchester, Illinois: Good News Publishers, 1967.

Tournier, Paul. *To Understand Each Other.* Atlanta: John Knox Press, 1967.

CPSIA information can be obtained at www.ICGtesting.com
Printed in the USA
LVOW110027080612

285098LV00002B/1/P